GET STARTED IN WRITING FOR CHILDREN

Lisa Bullard

Teach® Yourself

Get Started in Writing for Children

Lisa Bullard

Also available in ebook

For Vicki and Steve Palmquist – trusted teachers, faithful friends, endless encouragers

Acknowledgements

With huge thanks to my hundreds of writing students, who over the years have shared their dreams, their challenges, and their enthusiasm with me. I'm grateful for all that I've learned from you in return, and for all the ways you've inspired me. Know that each of you had an important hand in shaping this book and making it useful for a whole new 'classroom' of writers.

The author and publisher would like to express their thanks to the authors extracts of whose work appear in this book. These are listed in the References section at the end of this book.

Contents

About the author

I have been fortunate enough to build an exciting, challenging and creatively rewarding career in children's books. I have over 70 published titles to my credit, ranging from picture books to non-fiction to my most recent writing adventure, a middle-grade mystery novel. I worked in book publishing for 16 years, spending over five of those at one of the largest independent children's book publishers in the United States. For 14 years I've been teaching classes for adults who want to write for children. And, with another children's book author, I run a consulting service called Mentors for Rent – together, we provide advice and manuscript critiques to children's book writers at all stages of the process. I particularly enjoy the enthusiasm shown by brand-new writers, and I often feel I benefit as much as they do when I work with them!

One of the things I've learned from teaching and consulting is that there is not just one right approach to writing and creative success. But I have also discovered that my own experiences have given me many, many things to share with new writers that can help them avoid wrong turns. In this guide, I offer my own best writing tips and tactics, the kind of advice that I hope will help you quickly build your skills and gain confidence in your writing. My goal is for you to use what you find here to give you a solid start at writing for children, so that you are motivated to continue on past the pages of the guide to discover additional ways to succeed at your dream.

Lisa Bullard
www.lisabullard.com

Introduction: How to use this book

> 'Anyone who writes down to children is simply wasting his time. You have to write up, not down. Children are demanding. They are the most attentive, curious, eager, observant, sensitive, quick, and generally congenial readers on earth. They accept, almost without question, anything you present them with, as long as it is presented honestly, fearlessly, and clearly.'
>
> **Renowned children's book writer E.B. White**

So you want to write for children? You've come to the right place!

The people who write children's books are granted a privilege not shared by many: They are in the position to make a lasting impression on the lives of young people whom they will never meet in person.

Now you too have started a creative journey to explore whether that role of 'children's book writer' is a good fit for you – whether you might be one of those people who have it in themselves to make that kind of lasting impression on a still-growing mind and heart. Whether your goal is to write stories for your own children or for the world's children, this guide is a great starting point. It will teach you the basics of the children's book world and help you build writing skills and habits. It will provide helpful advice and resources, real-world examples and hands-on writing activities.

Those activities include shorter 'Snapshot' exercises, more in-depth 'Write' activities, and chapter-ending 'Workshop' examinations. Many of the activities in the early chapters are brainstorming exercises, designed to help you develop your skills and generate materials that will aid you in constructing a story. Since each chapter builds on the previous chapters, you will probably want to work your way through the book sequentially. By the end of the guide, if you've done your best to tackle all the presented activities, you'll find that you have a solid start – and perhaps even have finished – a story for young people!

Make sure to keep all of the activities you do throughout the guide in an easy-to-locate place, whether in a designated notebook or in a special folder on your computer. Later activities will sometimes ask you to refer to earlier activities, and you want them to be easy to find.

Every writer has their own approach. What you learn here will provide a great foundation as you take your first steps into writing for children, and will remain a useful reference source as you continue to identify your own best writing approach and stretch yourself through creating future stories.

The first step in pursuing your dream

People come to writing for children in different ways. Possibly you have had the ambition for many years but have only now found the confidence or time to try your hand at it. Or maybe you have worked with children and books as a teacher or librarian and now want to try writing yourself. Perhaps you've been sharing stories (those written by others or your own) with your children or grandchildren, and have decided that writing a book looks like fun.

However you've reached this step, it's likely that you'll discover, or have already discerned, the same thing that many others have found: the fact that these books target young readers doesn't mean they're easy to write. In fact, the opposite is true; children's books are challenging to write and challenging to get published, and the world of children's book writing has grown even more complex in the past few years.

A whole new world

Books written specifically for children have been around for hundreds of years. But many early books were intended to teach children lessons rather than to provide reading pleasure. Even today, a significant portion of the children's book market is devoted to non-fiction books that support what is taught in classrooms.

But while non-fiction provides many opportunities, the reality is that most writers who are first testing the children's book waters want to write stories, the kind of stories that children will love and remember for life. So the primary focus of this book is story writing, ranging from picture books for very young listeners to complex novels for teenagers. We will touch on some other possibilities in the final chapter, so as you work through the information and writing exercises found in these pages, keep in mind that much of the information you find will apply to any kind of writing for children.

More than the content of children's books has changed over the years. School curriculum guidelines regularly shift and affect what books are purchased and published. School and library budgets continue to decline. Children seem to have less down-time and more forms of entertainment fighting for their attention than ever before.

New technologies have had a serious impact on what and how children read as well. Technologies have changed the book production process, spurred the growth of online retailers, generated an ebook marketplace, and created social media marketing possibilities. There are additional and easier self-publishing opportunities. More children's books are available in more formats than ever before. But rather than taking power away from writers, this has made wordsmiths more necessary than ever. Writers are the people who create the content, and everything follows from that. It all starts with you: a writer and his or her idea, expressed through your unique writer's voice!

But within the last two decades, there has been one change that no children's book writer can ignore. That is the exponentially different level of expectations placed on today's children's books: the anticipation that each year there will be blockbuster hits. These are the kinds of books or series that generate their own merchandising franchises and reach far beyond books into movies, action figures and other licensed products. Certainly, there were successful children's books before the mid 1990s. But most children's book publishers were relatively low-key, staffed by editors who were passionate about children's books but didn't face extreme pressure for sky-rocketing sales numbers.

Then a certain boy wizard – followed by sparkly vampires and kick-butt girls surviving a variety of dystopias – made publishers ramp up their expectations to a heightened level. Mega-bestselling series like 'Harry Potter', 'Twilight' and the 'Hunger Games' created a radically different environment for children's books. Those titles and others have proven that books written for young people can become publishing's hottest properties. Writers have had to step up their game to take part in this more competitive world. There's still high demand for innovative projects and stellar writing, but writers are now expected to also be incredibly market savvy and to build promotional platforms for themselves as a matter of course. That's why, along with advice about the craft of writing, this book also helps you understand the children's book marketplace, and how you can engage in it. It's a new reality for children's book writers, but also an exciting one.

I can tell you from first-hand experience that, along with the challenges inherent in being a writer today, there are true opportunities and thrilling moments that make all of the hard work worth it. Perhaps that payoff for you will be the look on the face of a child you love when you present her with a story you wrote just for her. But if you are hoping for a bigger audience, you should know that, despite the complexities, every year there are still many new writers who experience the joy of seeing their name on the cover of their first book. Editors are driven to lay claim to the honour of being the 'person who discovered the next J.K. Rowling'. And debut writers consistently win major awards and honours. Persistence, enthusiasm and the kind of insider knowledge that you will find in these pages are all important tools as you pursue your dream. You are on the right path – a path I recognize from my own personal experience.

The workshop

This guide is designed as a 'teach yourself' tool. It will work as if you are taking one of my children's book writing classes, listening to lectures, participating in discussions, following through on writing exercises – and, finally, pausing regularly to evaluate and improve your own work. That is where the workshops come in. You will find that each chapter culminates in one of these workshops, just as many creative writing programmes in educational settings are structured around a workshop approach.

Each workshop is your chance to stop, critically examine one of the writing activities you have carried out, and, with the aid of the provided questions, to go back and revise your work before you move on to the next writing step. Don't skip this important part of the process! In this way, you will be reinforcing your newfound skills even as you learn them. The goal is to help you build your writing savvy as you go, internalizing each chapter's learning through this thoughtful review and application of what you have taken in. Developing the ability to assess your own work with an objective eye will be critical to your writing success. The workshops are key to helping you develop that skill.

The experience of tackling the workshops and reading through this guide will challenge you and, I hope, inspire you – just as you hope to inspire young readers with your words. Approach the process thoughtfully, with an attitude of playfulness, and with a willingness to stretch yourself, and you may be amazed to discover the power of the stories that will emerge.

So: let's get started in writing for children!

Icons

Here's your key to the different types of exercise and features in the book:

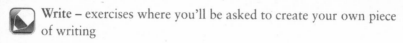 **Write** – exercises where you'll be asked to create your own piece of writing

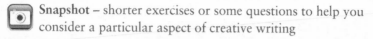 **Snapshot** – shorter exercises or some questions to help you consider a particular aspect of creative writing

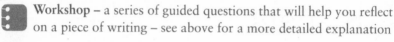 **Workshop** – a series of guided questions that will help you reflect on a piece of writing – see above for a more detailed explanation

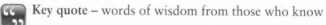 **Key quote** – words of wisdom from those who know

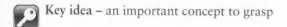 **Key idea** – an important concept to grasp

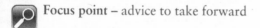 **Focus point** – advice to take forward

1

Reflect on your readers

The books we read as children can leave a potent imprint on us. Even decades later, we often remember details about the stories that mattered most to us as young people. And as those who write for children discover, it's thrilling to have that kind of impact on a child by creating a book that they love!

Children's author Heather Vogel Frederick

'There's something special about the books we fall in love with when we're young. We carry them with us in our hearts for the rest of our lives.'

A remembered read

Think back to your childhood and try to remember a favourite book. Write a paragraph describing the book and your experience with it. You might consider the following questions as you write:

- Did someone else read it to you, or did you read it alone?
- What did you love so much about that particular book?
- Can you remember any sensory details such as the feeling or the look of the book?
- For what span of ages did you think of that book as your favourite?
- Have you treasured that book for many years – maybe even shared it with your own children – or had you forgotten about it until this question?

What a difference a year or two makes

Don't be fooled – just because children's books are for young readers, they are no simpler to write than books for adults. But writing for children IS different from writing for adults. Not only will you shape young people with your writing, but young people will help shape your writing in return! Your audience will likely have an impact on some stage of your writing process, and they'll definitely influence the way the book is published. Fiction writers for adults don't have to stop and ask, 'Will a 34-year-old woman be able to grasp this concept?' But when you're writing for children, at some point you need to consider, 'Will a three-year-old understand this story?' Or, 'Will a six-year-old who has just learned to read be able to decipher this word?' Or, 'How will an eleven-year-old deal with this level of violence?' The way you answer questions like those may very well have a big impact on how you write your story.

It's almost as if your readers are peeking over your shoulder as you tap away at your keyboard. Sure, there are stages in the writing process when you'll write without an active awareness of those future fans. But the age, reading ability and developmental stage of your audience will have a significant impact on your finished book. Even a year or two can make a substantial difference in a child's ability to process certain words and concepts. So, in this chapter, we'll dig deeper into the world of children's books by looking at the way publishers divide readers into age categories.

Time machine

Imagine you have stepped into a time machine, and it has transported you back to the age of five. Everything you've learned or experienced since that age has been wiped clear from your memory. All you know and understand is what you knew and understood as a five-year-old. Close your eyes and let yourself sink into remembering what it felt like to be 'waist-high' in the adult world.

Once your eyes are open again, briefly answer the following questions the way you believe your five-year-old self would have answered them. Go with your gut impulse; don't overthink your answers!

- What scares you most?
- What do you keep secret?
- Whom do you most want to spend time with?

Once you've answered, step back into the time machine. Jump ahead to the age of ten. Some things will have changed since you were five. Answer those same three questions the way your ten-year-old self might have answered.

When your ten-year-old self has finished answering, jump ahead to age 15. Answer the three questions once again.

Look over all of your answers. What do you notice about the difference a few years can make in childhood?

The right book at the right time

Children are constantly changing, and the books that intrigue them change with their age. Those who connect children and books sometimes talk about it as the right book at the right time. When the match is a good one, it can lead to that powerful connection between a child and a favourite book. A mismatch – a book that's too hard to read, or covers content the child considers confusing or disturbing, boring or babyish – is a missed opportunity to grow a reader. So book publishers separate children's books into categories based on general age groups and reading ability. The categories work as a starting point to help make the matches between books and readers more successful. That way, when Grandma arrives at the bookshop to buy a birthday present for her nine-year-old grandson, the bookseller can quickly help her narrow down her search.

It's key to remember that many children's book purchase decisions are made by adults. The younger the reader, the less likely it is that he chooses what to read without adult supervision of some sort. But the best book match is when the child is also excited about the book choice. All the partners in the matchmaking process – publishers, parents and teachers included – have a vested interest in finding easy ways to pair books with young readers who will love them.

That's where book categories enter in. The categories are a short-cut language designed to help pair the right book with the right reader. Publishers expect writers to understand the categories, and for the most part, to shape their books to fit them. Doing so makes it easier for the publisher to sell books, and without book sales, the whole system collapses. Remember the grandma looking for a good book for a nine-year-old? Just how long would she have shopped if the books for children, babies and teens were all randomly mixed into the books for adults?

But putting books into pre-established categories often makes writers nervous. Books, they argue, aren't just products to be stuck in a pre-labelled slot; they're also artistic representations! And of course that's true; that mix of art and business is one of the things that makes the world of publishing so unpredictable, and ultimately so exciting.

Harold D. Underdown,
The Complete Idiot's Guide to Publishing Children's Books,
3rd edition

'Book publishing lies in an interesting middle area between art and commerce, between pure self-expression and the manufacture of millions of such useful but generic items as pencils and bars of soap. There's room for creativity, but you need to find an audience (your market), and a publisher will help you do that.'

Why you will want to learn the categories

Alexandra Alter, 'See Grown-ups Read', *Wall Street Journal*

'Far from being an anomaly, "Harry Potter" paved the way for a new crop of blockbuster children's books that are appealing to readers of all ages.'

There are children's books that defy the categories and become treasured reads for all ages of book lovers – a trend that seems to be growing. But the basic categories still form the key platform for the way children's books are sold. Learning about the categories is one way you can start to think like a professional writer. Publishers will take you more seriously if you speak their language, and understanding the categories is a part of that. So don't think of the categories as a limitation; of course, readers can choose to read outside of their prescribed designation. Instead, think of the categories as helpful guides that direct children to the books that they are most likely to fall in love with.

There are nuances to each children's book category, which we'll touch on as we examine each one more closely. Not to mention that every child is unique and might not fit into a pre-labelled age slot, either. And there is room for great creativity within each of the categories. A book for pre-readers might feature fantastical talking animals, or a non-fiction examination of the ways that animals communicate. A novel for teenagers might take the shape of a mystery, science fiction, a romance or even a story constructed of a series of poems. Fiction, non-fiction and poetry are published within each category. If there is a genre that you would like to write – horror, historical fiction, fantasy – there are children's book categories where it might be a good fit.

Some writers discover that they have an intuitive knack for writing in a way that appeals to children of a particular age. Other writers will have to experiment and play for quite a while to find their voice as a writer for children; for those writers, studying the categories can prove enormously helpful and time-saving. Whichever type of writer you turn out to be, understanding the categories will become critical at some point if you want to submit your work for possible publication.

 ## Key idea

Children's book publishers rely on age group categories to help put their books into the hands of the readers who will most appreciate them. As a children's writer, you will need to learn and understand what each of these categories represent.

Basic children's book categories

Category	Ages	Brief description	Examples
Picture books	0–7	Short books with eye-catching illustrations throughout; they are meant to be read out loud by an adult to a child	*Where the Wild Things Are* by Maurice Sendak; *Amazing Grace* by Mary Hoffman
Easy readers (aka early readers, beginning readers)	5–8	Short books where the language is carefully controlled for developing readers to learn reading skills	*The Cat in the Hat* by Dr. Seuss; *Today I Will Fly* by Mo Willems
Chapter books	6–9	Fairly simple books that are broken into chapters; the content and language use are still relatively easy for newly independent readers	*Dinosaurs before Dark* by Mary Pope Osborne; *Horrid Henry* by Francesca Simon
Middle grade	8–12	Multi-layered stories or non-fiction concepts written for practised readers; more complex and sometimes more difficult content can work well if handled in a way that is appropriate for pre-teens	*Charlie and the Chocolate Factory* by Roald Dahl; *The London Eye Mystery* by Siobhan Dowd
Young adult (aka YA, Teen)	12 up	Compelling, often intense stories that usually feature the teen experience in some way; often considered 'edgy'	*Forever...* by Judy Blume; *The Hunger Games* by Suzanne Collins

Note: These are the conventional names of categories in the United States, but they may go by different titles in the UK and in other parts of the world.

Connecting with the categories

The ability to remember what it truly feels like to be a child of a particular age will make your writing relatable and compelling to young readers. Your stories will be infused with authenticity. You may discover that it's easier for you to slip back to one age over another. Some people find it easier to recapture their experiences as a small child; others can't remember that stage. Others have strong memories of being a teenager dealing with hormones and heartaches. It could be because that was an exciting time, or because it was full of unresolved emotions. Either way, if your emotions and memories of a certain age are still intense, that can be a signal that you are well suited to write for a children's book category that covers that age.

 Focus point

Young readers form deep attachments with the books they love best. One way a writer can help solidify that bond is to authentically recapture the mindset and emotions of a particular developmental stage.

 Where do you fit?

Look back at your answers for the 'time machine' writing exercise. Consider the following:

- What changes do you note when you compare how your answers changed from one age to another? Which of those changes reflect the universal experience of growing up? Which changes were particular to your childhood?
- Did any of your answers take you by surprise, or spark memories you'd forgotten?
- Was it easier for you to put yourself into the mindset of a five, ten or fifteen-year-old?
- Vivid memories, both good and bad, can generate powerful writing. Did the answers for one particular age resonate most with you, stimulating the most intense memories?

- You should have come up with nine total answers for the time machine exercise. Choose your favourite answer; the one that created a sense of excitement, or made you laugh, groan or tear up over the memory.
- Considering your age from that memory (five, ten or fifteen), choose the categories that match up with it from the category chart.
- If more than one category is a match for your memory age, choose the category that is most appealing to you as a writer.
- In a few paragraphs, write about the memory that answer evokes. Write in a way that you believe will appeal to a child who is that same age; in other words, if you chose a memory from age ten, write it for a ten-year-old reader. Keep the guidelines for your chosen category in mind as you write.

Picture books

Picture books are packed with illustrations and are often packaged in a large trim size to showcase the art. These books are meant for reading out loud to a small child nestling in a lap, snuggling in bed, or squirming through story time. The illustrations tell at least half the story, so part of the writer's job is to craft a manuscript with strong visual potential that will serve as a springboard for an illustrator's creative process.

There are a variety of types of picture books. Concept books introduce children to learning concepts such as the alphabet, counting or colours. Non-fiction picture books dig into topics ranging from biographies to scientific facts. There are picture book poetry collections and wordplay titles. Narrative picture books tell complete stories despite their very spare text. They might be fantastical, thoughtful or zany stories; many offer peeks into the everyday experiences of preschoolers. Humorous stories have been especially popular in recent years.

THE REAL PICTURE BOOK AUDIENCE

Publishers typically list their picture books for ages four to eight because they're hoping for school sales. However, the true picture book audience typically skews a bit younger; it is primarily pre-readers. For writing purposes, think of the picture book audience as babies through around age seven. That's because once children begin learning to read independently, they have a corresponding impulse to be seen as less babyish – and they seek out 'big-kid books' (books broken into chapters).

As for children under the age of four, there is a picture book subcategory called board books. They target the youngest audience, from babies up to age three. Board books are chunky books printed on stiff cardboard. Many board books actually begin as traditional picture books, so if you have a manuscript that targets children three or under, you are often better off trying to sell it initially to a publisher as a picture book.

KEY TIPS FOR PICTURE BOOK WRITERS

- **Keep it brief:** Almost all current editors encourage writers to target 1,000 or fewer words, or even better, under 550 words. Non-fiction books may run somewhat longer.
- **Write to inspire visuals:** Make your text lively and active, so that it inspires an illustrator. But let the illustrator determine most of the specifics of how things look.
- **Target pre-readers:** Choose topics, story ideas, characters and a playful approach to language that will have intense appeal for pre-readers.
- **Make sure that it reads well out loud:** Picture books should sound great when read out loud. Think about the rhythm of your language, sound effects, refrains and words that are fun to say.
- **It's OK to use higher-level vocabulary words:** Because adults are reading these books to children, it's OK to use more complex language where it adds to the richness of the read-aloud experience.

 Focus point

In great picture books, the writer's text and the illustrator's art create a rich partnership of images and words. It is the writer's job to inspire – rather than dictate to – the illustrator.

Easy readers

Key idea

The comprehensibility of an easy reader text is as critical as the content. That makes these titles deceptively tough to write well. It can prove surprisingly difficult to tell an engaging story with so many restraints on vocabulary choice and sentence length. Unless you have special training in reading comprehension, the easy reader category may not be the easiest place for you to start.

Also called 'early readers' and 'beginning readers', easy readers are written specifically for children who are still learning to read. The books serve the important function of reinforcing reading skills. The category targets an audience range from approximately five to eight years old, as it takes some children much longer to become proficient readers than others.

Easy readers are short books, often comprising only a few hundred words. Vocabulary is carefully controlled. Writers might repeat specific sounds as a reinforcing tactic. Sentences are kept short; the general advice is to hold them to ten words or fewer, if possible. The publisher will add illustrations that give readers clues to understanding harder words.

KEY TIPS FOR EASY READER WRITERS

- **Remember reading comprehension:** The key to writing for this category is making the text comprehensible – but still engaging – for children who are just learning to read.
- **Keep it simple:** Reading itself is already tough enough for these beginners. Choose topics that will appeal to children aged five to eight, and keep your approach simple and easy to follow.

RESOURCES WHEN WRITING FOR NEW READERS

It can be difficult to determine whether a specific word will be understandable to a new reader. The US-oriented *Children's Writer's*

Word Book is a great resource for this; it's a thesaurus-like reference book where you can look up a word and see the school level at which a child typically comprehends it. Then alternate word choices are suggested for various school levels.

Educators also consider reading level assessment tools to determine which books are a good match for their students' reading abilities. In the United States, one of the available assessment tools is Renaissance Learning's ATOS Book Level. Renaissance provides an easy online tool that writers can use to determine the ATOS level for their complete manuscript as well; it can be found at renlearn.com/atos/analyze.aspx?type=1. An ATOS Book Level of 1.1, for example, is what a student in the first month of first grade in the US school system (typically six years old) might be expected to readily handle as far as reading comprehension. You can also go to arbookfind.com / http://www.arbookfind.co.uk/ to find the ATOS Book Level for popular easy reader titles so that you can compare their scores to the text you've created.

If you talk with reading educators, you will quickly learn that they have strong opinions about the different assessment tools. I'm not qualified to endorse Renaissance Learning from an educator's perspective. I single it out simply because it is the tool that specific publishers have requested I use when writing for new readers – and because as a writer, I have found it an easy way to check my written draft for its approximate reading level.

The reading level you naturally write for

Write a one-paragraph description of your favourite food treat. Don't consider reading level; use the language and sentence construction that feels natural. Remember the first time you ate that food. Write about your treat in a way that will make readers' mouths water!

When you are finished, go to Renaissance Learning at renlearn.com/atos/analyze.aspx?type=3 and follow the instructions there, using your description as your sample text. This will determine your ATOS level for your snapshot passage. It will give you a sense of what reading level you naturally fall into when writing. When I did this for the paragraph above, it tested at the 6.2 ATOS level.

Now rewrite the description of your food treat, this time with reading level very much in mind. Work through the following steps:

- Highlight words that seem too difficult for new readers. Find simpler substitutes.
- If any sentences are longer than ten words, try to break them into smaller sentences.
- Return to the Renaissance Learning site and submit the revised version of your passage. How much have you reduced your reading level?

Chapter books

As children gain more confidence in their reading skills, they move on to chapter books. Just as the name implies, these are books that are broken into chapters, usually containing illustrations (but not the elaborate illustrations found in picture books). They target readers who are now reading independently, but who are still developing their reading skills. These children are ready for longer books that have somewhat more complex language and content than easy readers. Do take note that some easy readers are also broken into chapters – the difference is that easy readers are written explicitly for reading comprehension and are even simpler than chapter books. Chapter books serve an important function by keeping practising readers, typically ages six to nine, engaged and excited about books.

KEY TIPS FOR CHAPTER BOOK WRITERS

- **Stretch readers a bit, but not too much:** Chapter book writers can stretch beyond the tight vocabulary constraints governing easy readers. But writers for this category still need to be aware of age-appropriate reading levels and relatively simple-to-follow texts.
- **Make reading fun:** Parents and educators want to provide books to children this age that will make reading pleasurable rather than onerous. For the most part, focus on light-hearted or humorous stories, or non-fiction titles full of intriguing facts.

Middle grade books

Some of the most famous children's books ever written fall into the middle grade category. Titles like E.B. White's *Charlotte's Web* and the first book in J.K. Rowling's 'Harry Potter' series are known even to adults who pay little attention to the world of children's literature. These titles demonstrate that children's books are in no way 'dumbed-down' writing, simpler to write than books for adults. Instead, these are fully developed stories that hold a universal appeal, while written to particularly engage young readers.

Middle grade books target ages eight through twelve, and some people consider them the heart of the children's book market. Children in this range have grown to be more accomplished readers, and this gives middle grade writers the opportunity to create more complex, multi-layered books. Story concepts can be more complicated, characters can have more depth, the world of the story can be more intricate, plots can be less linear, language can be more challenging.

Middle grade novels also tackle a wide range of subjects. Humorous books are still a big hit with readers this age, but titles might take on difficult topics such as broken families, bullying or the death of a friend. In recognition of the target audience's ages, the books generally steer clear of extreme violence, sexual topics and swearing.

 ## Children's book luminary Madeleine L'Engle

'You have to write the book that wants to be written. And if the book will be too difficult for grown-ups, then you write it for children.'

KEY TIPS FOR MIDDLE GRADE WRITERS

- **These books can be more complex than those for younger readers:** Middle grade readers are ready for greater reading challenges and more complex subject matter.

- **Children are still the target audience:** Books for this age level can focus on tough topics, but keep in mind that the readers are still pre-teens.

Key idea

Although middle grade readers are ready for a more demanding reading experience, they may not be ready – or the gatekeepers who help them choose books (parents, librarians, teachers) may not believe they are ready – to tackle certain life experiences. Create stories that challenge them as readers, but don't push them to grow up too fast.

Young adult

Young adult author Stephanie Kuehn

'[W]hy YA? Or what makes YA different? My answer is this: YA asks the questions. And it's OK with not knowing the answers.'

Young adult, or YA, is the category name given to books targeting teenagers. It is not as simple as labelling all books with teen characters 'YA'. However, most YA titles do feature teen main characters. And while books targeting adults might also feature a teen character, in the case of YA books, the character (and the story) will still be rooted in an adolescent view of the world; they will not yet have progressed to an adult perspective.

The best way to get a true feeling for what makes a book YA is to read a wide variety of titles that fall into the category. More than anything, you will find that young adult books share a focus on story, a sense of immediacy, and an intense reading experience. Readers are made to feel a deep connection to a character who is being confronted with the especially strong emotions, drama and life-changing decisions that are part of the adolescent experience.

YA titles cover a wide range of genres and approaches, from gritty reality-based stories to paranormal romance to disturbing dystopian visions. Books may include edgier material that reflects YA's older readership: sexuality, violence and difficult topics such as suicide, rape and abuse. If something reflects actual teenage experience or teenage hopes and fears, it's potential material for a YA novel.

 Key idea

In recent years, YA has become one of the hottest categories in all of publishing, in part because of the many adult readers who have discovered how compelling these stories can be.

KEY TIPS FOR YOUNG ADULT WRITERS:

- **Authenticity counts:** Make sure to tap into your teenage emotions and immerse yourself in contemporary teen experiences and influences so that your characters come across as authentically teen (even if they are teen zombies or teen spies).
- **Create reader connections:** Whether it is feeling as if they are inside a particular fantasy world, swept up in an intense romance, or grappling with a jarring crisis, young adult readers want a sense of immediacy and connection, rather than distance and objectivity, from their reading experiences.
- **Think teen:** Adolescence is an intensely felt transitional time from childhood to adulthood. The first-time experiences and decisions that shape teenagers' lives also create powerful stories.

 Teen again

Think back to your teenage years and choose one of the important 'firsts' that you experienced (examples might include first job, first kiss, first break-up, first time driving a car, first party with no adult supervision). Describe the experience in a few paragraphs. As you write, push yourself to imbue your writing with a feeling of intensity. The goal is to recapture some of the strong emotions and experiences of those adolescent years.

Solidify your category consciousness

Each of the five children's book categories we've discussed represents a specific audience with different reading needs and preferences. A writer might choose to write about the same basic life experience for each of the five categories – but the stories would vary, often substantially, because of the different target audiences.

Here's an example. If the life experience that I've decided to write about is 'FIRST LOVE', then I might summarize five different possible approaches, based on the five categories, in this way:

- **Picture book:** a story about a four-year-old who has a crush on his preschool teacher, and the funny or sweet gifts he brings her each day to express his love.
- **Easy reader:** a story about a seven-year-old girl who has always been best friends with the little boy next door until something goes wrong. Focus on simple language and short sentences. Find a way to include a happy ending.
- **Chapter book:** a story about a nine-year-old who begins receiving notes from a secret admirer. Set it up as a fun mystery, with the character tracking down clues to discover the admirer's identify. Each brief chapter could reveal one new clue.
- **Middle grade:** a story about a 12-year-old whose father has deserted her family. Her friends are always talking about boys, and she secretly likes that nice guy in her school play. But the character struggles to determine if she can trust any boy, given her father's abandonment.
- **Young adult:** a story about a 17-year-old who has her first sexual relationship with her dying brother's best friend.

There are three other life experiences listed below. Consider each of those life experiences in light of the five categories. Brainstorm and then write a few notes describing how you could tackle these core experiences for each category, as I did above.

- Loss of an important relationship
- Going to a new school
- Making a bad choice

Are you experiencing category confusion?

The category breakdowns aren't absolute; the lines often blur as one category meets the next. Different publishers may define each category in a slightly different way. Books such as fantasy titles or graphic novels can be difficult to categorize. Don't let any of that throw you off. Now that you have these categories in your mind as you continue to write and read children's books, you'll find yourself gaining confidence in understanding what books belong in which category.

The key is to remember the reason for the categories in the first place: they are a tool for matching young readers to books that will offer them a successful and satisfying reading experience. Don't lose track of the fact that on the other side of the children's book you are writing there will hopefully one day be a child audience, and the rest will fall into place.

 Key idea

To succeed as a children's book writer, you should also be an avid children's book reader. Devour a broad assortment of children's books on an ongoing basis. Make sure to include many new titles alongside the classics. The more you read, the more likely you will discover the categories with which you especially resonate – not only as a reader, but also as a writer.

Regularly reading children's books will teach you as much about writing well for children as anything else you can do.

Stay open to possibilities

Sometimes writers simply don't know which audience, and therefore category, they want to target when they begin a project. That's perfectly OK. At some point you will want to identify that target audience, and for some writers it is enormously helpful to know it from the beginning. But if that doesn't happen to be the case for you, don't let it be the thing that keeps you from getting started.

Throughout the drafting process, there will be other opportunities for you to consider the target audience that will most appreciate the story you are driven to tell, and eventually you will decide on a category. You can fine-tune your manuscript to better suit that particular category when you turn to revising in Chapter 8.

And even those times when a writer does set out with a clear sense of his or her target audience, creativity can prove to be a tricky thing. The writing process can take unexpected turns, and a manuscript that was meant to fit one category can shift to be more appropriate for another. Be flexible: if your work seems to be shaping itself to be better suited for a different category, stay open to that possibility.

Workshop

1 Review

For the 'Where do you fit?' writing exercise, you shared a particular childhood memory, writing it with a specific children's book category in mind. Read over that piece now. Considering the additional information you have learned about the categories, rate yourself on how well you did at the following (1 being the lowest score, 10 being the highest):

- Vocabulary choices   1 2 3 4 5 6 7 8 9 10
- Complexity of the story   1 2 3 4 5 6 7 8 9 10
- Emotional intensity   1 2 3 4 5 6 7 8 9 10
- Subject matter appeal   1 2 3 4 5 6 7 8 9 10

2 Close-up

Vocabulary choices

- Do your vocabulary choices sound true-to-life for a child or teen of the age you were writing for?
- If you were writing for the easy reader or chapter book category, did your vocabulary choices reflect an appropriately young reading level?
- If you were writing for the picture book, middle grade or young adult category, were your vocabulary choices

varied and interesting for these more practised readers (remember that adults will read picture books to children)?

- What words could you change to create a satisfying reading experience that matches your chosen category's reading ability?

Choose alternate words or rewrite your sentences as necessary to strengthen your work, bearing in mind your responses to the questions above.

Complexity of the story

- If your story is for the picture book, easy reader or chapter book category, is it told in a simple, linear fashion?
- If your story is for the middle grade or young adult category, does it include more layers and depth?
- Depending on your category choice, what could you add or take away from your piece to make it a better complexity match for your audience?

Rewrite your work, making it more or less complex based on your responses to the questions above.

Emotional intensity

- Are the emotions in your story expressed the way that a child of that age would express them?
- If your story is for the picture book category, will preschool children relate to the emotions being experienced?
- If your story is for the easy reader or chapter book category, is it fairly light-hearted?
- If your story is for the middle grade or young adult category, is the emotional resonance a bit more intense (even for humorous stories)?
- Depending on your category choice, how might you increase or lessen the emotional intensity of your story?

Rewrite your work, making it more or less emotionally intense based on your responses to the questions above.

Subject matter appeal

What are the primary concerns of children in your chosen category?

- Is the subject matter of your story something that will appeal to readers of the suggested age ranges for your chosen category?
- Is there something you could change or add to make your subject matter more appealing to your target audience?
- Is there something you should delete from your story because your target audience won't be interested in it?

Rewrite your work, making the subject matter more appealing based on your responses to the questions above.

3 Re-review

Now read your revised work and re-rate the following from 1 to 10:

- Vocabulary choices   1 2 3 4 5 6 7 8 9 10
- Complexity of writing   1 2 3 4 5 6 7 8 9 10
- Emotional intensity   1 2 3 4 5 6 7 8 9 10
- Subject matter appeal   1 2 3 4 5 6 7 8 9 10

Where to next?

We've talked about the most distinguishing feature of children's books: their young audience. Next we move on to the tactics writers use to find successful children's book ideas. We'll talk about brainstorming and researching. We'll explore theme, which is the heart of your story. And you'll choose the idea that you'll pursue as you continue on your journey to writing a children's book!

2

Explore for ideas

One of the most common questions I hear about my writing is, 'Where do you get your ideas?' For me, finding ideas is rarely the problem; I usually have way too many of them. Ideas are everywhere; we just have to learn to recognize them. Sometimes the answer is as simple as a routine activity: I know writers who find their most interesting ideas while taking their morning walk or while commuting to work. For myself, I've often thought I should keep a grease pencil in the shower, because running water seems to make new ideas pop out on a regular basis! I even justify spending some time on my favourite social media forum, Pinterest, by keeping a 'YA World' board (pinterest.com/lisambullard/ya-world/), where I collect images that fit loosely around a still-vague notion I have for a young adult book.

Book ideas come in many forms. Fortunately, there is no one right way to conceive of a book concept. One idea might show up as a character whispering in your ear, so that you are compelled to uncover more of her story. Another idea might come about as an interesting storyline that tackles a specific subject, such as toddlers learning to share or the struggles of teen pregnancy.

An idea doesn't have to be fully fleshed out to be worth considering. It might be in the form of a half-formed memory, a brief sensory impression, or one side of an overheard conversation. The key is to pay attention to whether an idea sparks energy for you; if it triggers some kind of emotional response, or intrigues you enough to imagine what might come next, it's worth keeping on your 'Ideas List'.

My challenge often comes when it's time to sift through my many half-formed ideas to pinpoint the one that will work on several levels: that challenges me as a writer, that has enough substance to carry a story, and that has potential audience appeal. Often I have to play with the idea for quite a while, trying to connect it to other half-formed ideas to see whether they fit together like puzzle pieces, and then perhaps writing a draft or two, before I know if the idea has the legs to work on these multiple levels.

Sometimes an idea doesn't prove to have carrying power. Most writers have a drawer or computer full of story starts that they didn't finish for one reason or another. And sometimes even years later, you realize you've now learned what you needed to know as a writer to bring a long-ago-abandoned idea to fruition!

Having an over-abundance of ideas on hand is a gift for a writer. If one fizzles, you then have ten more to explore. That's why, in this chapter, we'll try an array of brainstorming tactics and suggestions for researching ideas, with the goal of generating an Ideas List that you can draw on as you continue to practise your writing skills. Along with brainstorming ideas, we'll examine the role of theme in a story, and discuss how you can narrow down your Ideas List to select the one that you want to tackle first.

Start an Ideas List

Brainstorming is a key stage in the writing process. Ideally, you will want to be wildly creative in the brainstorming stage, not pausing to edit or critique your ideas but instead pushing yourself to think outside the box. Even an outlandish idea can spur a wonderful story!

And whether you're a person who lives for making lists or not, you'll want to devise a system for recording and organizing your ideas as they occur to you. Much as we're sure that today's brainstorm won't be lost, it's all too often buried under another great idea tomorrow. Don't lose this precious commodity that could lead to your next great story.

You can keep a simple handwritten Ideas List in a large notebook. You can jot down each concept on a separate index card, adding further details as your idea grows or you think of connected ideas. You can keep a running list in a computer file. There's no one right answer; the key is to set up a system that's simple enough that you'll keep it up to date, and that's easy to scan when you're looking for inspiration. And you may want to also carry a small notebook, recording device or cell phone with a note-taking app when you leave the house. Ideas don't always wait to pop out when we're conveniently situated in front of our home computer or organizing system.

Choose the organizational system you'd like to try first, buy the necessary materials, and put the basics of your Ideas List into place.

Some kind of idea brought you to this guide, and you don't want to lose track of it as you generate many more ideas throughout this chapter. So once you have your Ideas List set up, take some time to jot down all of the ideas you already have in mind for a children's story. Then remember to keep coming back to add to your Ideas List whenever you have a new idea. You might not technically be in a brainstorming stage of writing when the idea occurs to you, but you want to quickly capture the kernel of each new idea when it is fresh – and then go back to whatever else you were focused on. An Ideas List is always a work-in-progress.

Writing from real life

 ## Award-winning young adult author Pete Hautman

'[M]ost of my YA work is drawn directly from those five or six boring, embarrassing, mind-numbing, awkward, adolescent years – it's all still there in a midden at the back of my head. I mine that midden – my credit balance – on a daily basis.'

Writers often draw on actual experiences from their own childhoods, or from the lives of young people they know, for inspiration. Sometimes writers explore a general life experience that a large number of readers have lived through. This might include being bullied, going through a parental divorce, or surviving a first break-up. At other times, writers draw on something that fewer readers have directly experienced, such as growing up in an immigrant family or living with a disability.

The 'Harry Potter' series is a good example of how a writer tapped into both universal and unique elements to create a successful story. Only a small portion of J.K. Rowling's readership will be childhood orphans, and even fewer will wake up one day to discover that they've been singled out as a famous wizard. But almost all of her readers can relate to the feeling of not quite belonging at some point in their life, or of wishing that they were somehow secretly special. Rowling taps into universal emotions through the specific experiences of a compelling character.

Universal and unique

Choose an experience from your own childhood, or the life of a child you know well. Select one that seems like a relatively common childhood experience. Examples might include the death of a pet, a first day at school, or a time you failed at something that was important to you. Write a few paragraphs describing the experience. Focus both on the emotions of the experience (what makes it universal) and the particulars of how it played out in your own life (what makes it unique).

Now choose a different experience, one that seems more specific to your own life (or the life of a child you know well); choose something that a higher percentage of children will not have experienced. Write a few paragraphs describing this experience. Focus both on the emotions of the experience (what makes it universal) and the particulars of how it played out in your own life (what makes it unique).

Reveal emotional truth

A real-life event can be a powerful jumping-off point for a story. But sometimes when writers are drawing on personal experience, they become overly focused on recreating every detail of what really happened. Real-life stories don't always fit deftly into a storyline full of tension and suspense; what really happened may include many moments that are, in fact, distractions or even boring when you're recreating the story.

Unless you've deliberately set out to write a non-fiction work such as a biography or memoir, your job is to tell the best possible story, and you have permission to deviate from reality. Be willing to let go of the minute (but disposable) details of what actually happened, and instead work to highlight the emotional truth you learned through that life experience.

What if?

It's easy to fall into making assumptions that our story must go a certain way (such as 'it must describe what really happened'). But asking yourself 'what if' pushes you to invite surprises into your work – the kind of surprises that make your writing feel fresh and original.

Choose one of the two pieces you wrote for the 'Universal and unique' snapshot activity. Reread the piece, and then write a series of ten questions – all starting with 'What if…' – that change the story in some way. Perhaps you might ask, 'What if the child in the story was the opposite gender?' Or, 'What if the story resolved in a completely different way?' Even, 'What if it turns out that one of the characters is a ghost/alien/shape-shifter?' Be creative and think beyond the obvious!

Once you have ten 'what if' questions, rewrite your piece incorporating at least one of the new elements from that 'what if' list.

Key idea

One of the most useful of all questions a writer can ask is 'What if?' Push yourself to explore the unexpected possibilities in your ideas.

Follow the facts

Book ideas can pop up anywhere. It pays to be on alert at all times. Reading a quirky trivia list, immersing yourself in a serious non-fiction title for adults, or spending some time wandering the Internet can pay off with an intriguing story notion. A news article might spur an idea for a geographic setting for a new story. A reference to 'this day in history' might motivate you to explore a specific time period through writing historical fiction.

In the case of my middle grade mystery novel, I was researching unusual animals for a non-fiction book for very young children when I stumbled across information about the walking catfish. If its pond becomes toxic or dries up, this fish actually leaves the water and 'walks' across ground to find a new and more nourishing pond. I was enthralled by this example of a true 'fish out of water', and it became the foundation for my human character's quest in *Turn Left at the Cow*.

In your Ideas List, make sure to include quirky facts that you might incorporate into a story.

In the know

Don't forget to consider areas in which you have some level of expertise. You don't have to be a world authority on a subject to mine it for story ideas. Here are some possible starting points:

- Your formal education
- Factual topics on which you've read deeply
- Work experiences
- Your hobbies
- Organizations to which you belong
- Travel
- Life experiences

Some areas of your expertise might make interesting topics for non-fiction children's books (which we'll discuss in further detail in Chapter 10). But they can also serve as the building blocks for fiction. Perhaps your experience as the parent of an autistic child has given you an idea for a young character who processes life in a way that is different from her peers. Maybe you've decided to send your teenage character off to work as an intern in the industry in which you're employed. Perhaps you've realized it could be intriguing to make your character an exchange student in the fascinating corner of the world where you regularly travel.

Get schooled

Schools are an important market for children's books, so publishers pay careful attention to how their publications fit into curriculum standards. In reverse, you can mine curriculum standards for children's book ideas. Do an Internet search for the curriculum standards for your home country or region, and then narrow down your search to the age levels you are interested in targeting with your books. What specific topics are children studying at those age levels? When do they study the historical time period in which you want to set your story? Are there values-based concepts that are included in the curriculum (perhaps something about respecting diversity or an anti-bullying unit)? All of these are potential book ideas.

Of course, other writers are also aware of the school curriculum, so many individuals have studied these same sources. When you hit on a topic that's of high interest to you personally, do some research to see what competing books already exist on this topic. Is there an interesting angle or perspective you could take to ensure that your book concept feels fresh and original?

Don't overlook teachers and librarians as another direct source for ideas. Those who work to put books in the hands of children on a regular basis usually have a clear sense of what ideas will be most appealing, and where there are holes in terms of what is already available on the bookshelves. Stop in at a library and ask what book topics and genres (such as fantasy or mysteries) children most often request (both for pleasure reading and to use as aids for schoolwork). Make sure to add the answers you receive to your Ideas List.

Learn more about child development

As we discussed in Chapter 1, writing for children includes targeting a specific age range of children – which also demands some understanding of the developmental stages that children move through as they grow up. Some children's book writers are in the fortunate position of having a professional background that includes child development training, or they work with children on a daily basis. If that's the case for you, don't underestimate what a bonus this is! Many other writers have first-hand experience with child development through their role as a parent. But don't despair if this isn't the case for you. You may then want to do some research, perhaps through the many helpful child development guides written for parents and caregivers. These provide a look at what to expect at each age level. You may want to keep a running list of milestones and struggles, listed by age, on your Ideas List.

The Internet is a handy tool as well. For example, a quick Google search led me to this BabyCenter website page (babycenter.com/0_milestones-25-to-36-months_1496593.bc) that lists milestones for children ages 25–36 months. Scanning the list, I quickly came up with the following basic book ideas to add to my own list:

- Fears about monsters
- Can pedal a tricycle
- Throws tantrums
- Learning to share and take turns
- Moving to a real bed
- Toilet training

You may also want to develop your spy skills as a hands-on way to learn about child development stages. You never want to cross the line into scary stalker, of course; don't interact directly with children unless you have their parents' permission to do so. Respect boundaries at all times. However, at various times I've volunteered to do the school run for a friend, sat in the back at a public library story time, and hung out in a coffee shop popular with teenagers. Each of these gave me the opportunity to tap into the conversational patterns, behaviours and preoccupations for children of a particular target age.

Key idea

Children enjoy seeing their own lives and preoccupations mirrored in the books they read.

Take a cue from pop culture

Just as books target children of various age categories, so do television shows, magazines, video games, toys, movies, music and a wide array of other products and cultural experiences. You will want to study the range of offerings for children in the age categories for which you want to write. These products will immerse you in some of the influences shaping your potential young readers, and give you insights into what the top-level marketing people at major corporations have identified as commercially viable trends for marketing to children (or their parents).

As we discussed in Chapter 1, you shouldn't fail to immerse yourself in the most current books being published for children and teens. Reading these new offerings will likely inspire your own book ideas – along with showing you current book trends that will root you in the world of contemporary children's book publishing (an important background to have when it comes time to submit your own work to publishers). You will also want to familiarize yourself with other books that tackle the same concepts that keep popping up on your own Ideas List, so that you can think about how you might tackle the subjects in your own unique way. Also take a look at the books that have recently won the major children's book awards – they are a signal of the types of titles that are being deemed most critically worthy in today's children's literature universe.

If writing a book that has high sales potential is one of your goals, you will want to pay particular attention to book bestseller lists. Remember, of course, that reading tastes can prove fickle and unpredictable. You don't want to set out to produce a clone of today's bestseller; by the time you've finished writing your novel, selling it to a publisher, and seen it through the publishing process, zombies (or whatever is the current trend) may have run their course. But whether or not zombies stand the test of time, your book will be most successful if you find a way to put your own unique, personal spin on it. It can also be very difficult to carry yourself through the long process of writing a saleable book if you don't feel inspired by the subject matter – so choose a trend that appeals to you personally as well.

But those warnings don't mean that you should ignore what's selling well if you hope to make a commercial success out of writing. If you keep studying the bestseller lists, you'll note that certain trends tend to have staying power; publishers know this better than anyone, and they build their businesses based on what's selling now, and what they predict will sell in three years. Vampires may have lost their bite, but young adult books that feature paranormal romance are still popular. And each new generation of little boys will predictably laugh uproariously at 'gross-out' humour. Can you think of an idea that provides a fresh take on a proven trend? Are there perennially popular concepts that appeal to you as a writer?

As you begin to immerse yourself in the bigger world of children's books – something we'll talk about in more detail in Chapter 9 – you will also discover that certain societal issues or concerns can initiate children's book trends. For example, publishers and educators may suddenly be experiencing a heightened awareness of the need for diverse characters in children's books. This may spur ideas and opportunities that you can add to your Ideas List.

Key idea

It's important to remember that publishing is a business that depends on selling books as products. Publishers have to stay ahead of trends and second-guess reading tastes to survive. Writers who want to sell their work are well served to track what sells best to their hoped-for readership as well.

Q&A brainstorm activity

This brainstorming activity extends our focus in Chapter 1 – the notion that your book will someday become the perfect read for a child of a particular age – the right book at the right time.

- Choose an age of child for whom you are interested in writing.
- Then ask a broad question about the preferences of children that age – for example, 'What do ten-year-olds love?' or 'What is important in a five-year-old's world?'

- Generate seven answers for that broad question.
- Then take one of the answers (whichever one sparks energy for you) and reframe it as a new question.
- Generate seven answers for that new question.
- Continue in this fashion, turning one item from each list of answers into a new question, and coming up with seven more answers. Your questions will become more specific and focused, and so will your answers. Keep going until you reach a level where you feel you've generated an intriguing list of specific and intriguing details. And if one branch comes to a dead-end, you can always try another!

This activity description may sound complicated, but it's actually pretty straightforward. Here's an example to show you how easy this brainstorming approach can be:

Broad question: *What is important in a five-year-old's world?*
- Family
- Pets
- Toys
- Play
- School
- Friends
- Holidays

I posed the new question: *What holidays do five-year-olds love?*
- Christmas
- Purim
- Eid al-Fitr
- Birthdays
- Valentine's Day
- Easter
- Halloween

I posed the new question: *What makes Halloween so special?*
- Trick-or-treat
- Costumes
- Candy
- Being out at night

- Spooky stuff
- Interacting with neighbours
- The unexpected

I posed the new question: *How is Halloween about things not being what they seem on the surface?*

- People are hidden under costumes.
- Things look very different in the dark.
- We celebrate the spooky side of life.
- The seasons are in a time of transition.
- Decorations make the common look unfamiliar.
- It's OK to ask strangers to give us candy.
- We wander around outside in the night-time.

That last question, 'How is Halloween about things not being what they seem on the surface?' and the corresponding list of answers, provides several intriguing elements to pursue in a story. And in fact, my picture book *Trick-or-Treat on Milton Street* features a little boy who is surprised to discover that his new stepfather and his new neighbourhood are not at all what they seem to be at first glance.

Try this Q&A approach for yourself, and see what intriguing book ideas you come up with. If you don't like the first list you come up with, try going down a different branch of your Q&A 'tree'.

Should you teach a lesson?

Focus point

Writing from a sense of conviction can create deeply powerful stories. However, you definitely want to avoid writing in a way that feels preachy or moralizing.

Some writers develop story concepts around morals or lessons about good versus bad behaviour. Perhaps you have a passionate conviction that humankind is destroying the planet, or you want to spare young readers from making the mistake that you did when you got caught shoplifting or cheating on a school test.

Can you convert your strong convictions into compelling stories? Absolutely! But make sure that the lesson emerges through the action and conflict built into your story, and not through a moment when someone (typically an adult) in the story interrupts the action to lecture the reader. Children are lectured on a regular basis about how they should behave and what they should believe. They'll quickly tune out a writer who has climbed on to a soapbox and is trying to teach them a lesson.

It's fine to tell a story where readers will recognize for themselves that the character has had to pay the consequences of making a bad choice, but those consequences should emerge in an organic way as part of what unfolds in the story. Don't be didactic.

Is your idea a 'big idea'?

Debbie Notari, Education Portal website

'The theme in a story is its underlining message, or "big idea". What critical belief about life is the author trying to convey...?'

Theme often emerges as bigger than a simple moralistic message. Theme is the deeper meaning that unifies the story; it is some truth or insight about human experience that the reader will carry away with them – perhaps without even consciously realizing that they have internalized that insight.

Theme is more abstract than the subject of the story. Your story's subject might be a child who struggles with a severe disfigurement; your theme for the same story might be that human beings all have the same needs, despite their surface differences.

A story may have multiple themes, especially if it's for older children. Stories for younger children are likely to have fewer themes as part of the mandate to keep them simple enough for developing readers.

You don't have to identify your story's theme before you start writing. In fact, there are times when you won't be able to articulate a clear theme for your story even after investing a great deal of time in it! That's perfectly OK.

But if your book idea arrives in the form of a possible theme, that can be a great help for you. You can use your theme as a unifying element for your story, measuring everything you might include against the theme to see if it truly belongs in the story. But beware of the same risk that you face when you're writing with a lesson to teach; you can become so focused on the theme that the story feels heavy-handed and didactic. The key is to allow the theme to emerge through all the elements of the story, rather than explicitly stating it as a message.

Dear Reader

Think of some deep truth or insight about life or the experience of being human that you would like to share with a young reader. Or to phrase it differently, if you were to have a book published, what is the most important 'takeaway' that you'd want to impart to your young audience?

Focusing on that takeaway, write a letter to a child of the age that you chose for the 'Q&A brainstorm' activity. Address your letter to 'Dear Reader'. This is your chance to explore a possible theme, or focus, for a story, something meaningful that you'd like to pass along to the next generation.

Which idea should you pursue first?

Award-winning children's writer Marion Dane Bauer

'When I am working with students of all ages who want to write but can't find what they want to write, I always begin by asking them what they like to read, what they like to do, what excites them, scares them, makes them sad. It's a search that begins with the superficial and moves tentatively toward that deep inner place where, suddenly, something feels important. It is that feeling of importance that energizes a story.'

At this point, you likely have several story ideas vying for your attention. So how do you choose which one to pursue first? One key piece of advice is to follow the idea that has the most energy for you.

What does that look like? Ask yourself: Which idea sparks the most creative enthusiasm for me right now? Which one gives me the sense that I can't wait to jump in and begin exploring the possibilities that the concept offers?

 Focus point

Writers who are in it for the long term face a lot of rejection and hard work (and most often, not nearly enough financial compensation). They continue to write because of the passion they feel for it, and for the creative buzz that comes when you bring a compelling idea to life.

Prioritizing based on target audience

Sometimes, you will prioritize one idea over another because of the audience category it best suits. Some ideas can be adapted to fit any age reader; you could tell a story about the challenges of moving to a new town or a fight with a friend for any age. Then you will want to think through how you would tackle that same topic differently for a three-year-old versus a thirteen-year-old. This is one way that having a basic knowledge of child development can be helpful. Studying how children of different ages process death, for example, might heavily influence whether you write a picture book about the death of a pet or a middle grade novel about the death of a parent.

Some ideas are less general and point more specifically towards a particular audience. If your 'fight with a friend' story morphs into a story about a broken romance, then your audience will skew towards the older children's book categories. A tough concept like drug addiction is better suited to an older audience as well. But your cute bunny family is obviously a better fit for a picture book than a YA title.

Remember to be open to the possibility that even though you start out believing an idea is best suited for one children's book category, you might realize through working with the idea that it is actually a better match for a different category. And you may not have any idea about category at all in this early stage; then the process of shaping your idea can help you identify your target audience.

Choose your top ideas

Review your Ideas List. Then choose your three top ideas: the ones that have the most energy for you right now, and that best fit the category or categories you are interested in tackling as a writer at the moment.

For each of your top three ideas, write four or five paragraphs that expand further on it. Write possibilities for how you will approach each idea, ask yourself questions about it, imagine different directions you might take your concept. This is your chance to play around with each of these top ideas, to explore each of them further before you choose which one you will tackle first.

Can you work on different ideas simultaneously?

Some writers choose to focus on only one project at a time, writing it from start to finish before beginning a new one so as not to disrupt their focus. Other writers believe that they are more productive if they work with multiple ideas simultaneously. This second approach has proven very effective for me if I stagger a select few projects so that they are at different stages of the writing process: researching my idea, early draft, revision, submitting to publishers. That way if I stall out on one idea, I can shift to another that has more energy for me at the moment. As you gain writing confidence, you might want to try this 'multiple projects at different stages' approach.

Workshop

1 Review

For the 'Choose your top ideas' exercise, you explored three of your book ideas in more depth. Look back at what you wrote and choose which idea you want to tackle first as you continue to explore a children's book project using this guide. Since most of this guide focuses on story writing, for the purpose of moving forward you should choose a story concept (rather than an idea for a collection of poetry, for example). If you know at this point, also identify the children's book category you will target with this idea – picture book or YA, for example – realizing that this may shift as you continue to work on your project.

Considering all that you have learned so far, rate your idea on the following (1 being the lowest score, 10 being the highest):

- My idea will appeal to and be relatable for children or teenagers. [1] [2] [3] [4] [5] [6] [7] [8] [9] [10]
- My idea taps into something universal about the human experience. [1] [2] [3] [4] [5] [6] [7] [8] [9] [10]
- My idea has an element that is fresh or unique. [1] [2] [3] [4] [5] [6] [7] [8] [9] [10]
- My idea has the potential to portray an emotional truth. [1] [2] [3] [4] [5] [6] [7] [8] [9] [10]
- My idea is big enough to carry me through an entire story. [1] [2] [3] [4] [5] [6] [7] [8] [9] [10]

2 Close-up

My idea will appeal to and be relatable for children or teenagers

- Is your idea something that will appeal to children or teenagers?
- What would make your idea even more relatable to young people?

- Considering the broader context of your idea, what should you steer away from because it is not age appropriate?

Bearing in mind your response to the questions above, what could you do to make your idea more appealing and relatable for children or teenagers? Add your thoughts to the paragraphs you wrote for this idea in the 'Choose your top ideas' activity.

My idea taps into something universal about the human experience

- Would children from different parts of the world be able to relate to some element of your idea?
- Would children from different socio-economic backgrounds be able to relate to some element of your idea?
- Does your idea have a 'timeless' quality – will children 30 years from now find something relatable about it?

Bearing in mind your response to the questions above, what could you do to make your idea a stronger reflection of the universal human experience? Add your thoughts to the paragraphs you wrote for this idea in the 'Choose your top ideas' activity.

My idea has an element that is fresh or unique

- Does your idea feel generic or too broad?
- Does your idea seem too similar to other books you've read?
- Does your idea contain some attention-grabbing element?
- Is there something about your idea that might make someone say, 'I was aware that children experienced this, but I've never thought about it in quite this way (or from this point of view) before'?

Bearing in mind your response to the questions above, what could you do to make your idea feel more unique and original, or to offer a fresh take on something? Add your thoughts to the paragraphs you wrote for this idea in the 'Choose your top ideas' activity.

My idea has the potential to portray an emotional truth

- Is there potential for your idea to reveal something on a deeper level about the human experience?
- Even if your idea is not real (it is based on fictional events or perhaps even a fantasy), does it tap into emotional truths that will ring true for readers?
- Consider the children's book category that you think you might tackle using this idea. Are the emotional struggles that you imagine drawing out in your story the kind of emotional struggles that drive a child of that age range? (For example, a very small child might be struggling with intense separation anxiety from Mom, while a high school student might struggle more with self-esteem issues around peers.)

Bearing in mind your response to the questions above, what could you do to give your idea more emotional resonance? To better suit it to the key emotions experienced by readers in your possible target book category? Add your thoughts to the paragraphs you wrote for this idea in the 'Choose your top ideas' activity.

My idea is big enough to carry me through an entire story

- Do you still feel a genuine sense of enthusiasm or excitement about pursuing this idea?
- Did you struggle to write four or five paragraphs about your idea, or did your thoughts flow easily?
- As you work through these workshop questions, does your enthusiasm for the idea grow?
- Although you don't yet know all the elements of your story, do you sense that there are lots of possibilities for how you might continue to build on this idea?

If you find that you are struggling to generate enthusiasm or possibilities for this idea, this is a good time to reconsider and choose an alternate idea. Review your other top choices, or return to your Ideas List and pull out another possibility. Then work your way through this workshop exercise using your new idea instead.

3 Re-review

Now read your revised work and re-rate the following from 1 to 10:

- My idea will appeal to and be relatable for children or teenagers
  1 2 3 4 5 6 7 8 9 10
- My idea taps into something universal about the human experience
  1 2 3 4 5 6 7 8 9 10
- My idea has an element that is fresh or unique
  1 2 3 4 5 6 7 8 9 10
- My idea has the potential to portray an emotional truth
  1 2 3 4 5 6 7 8 9 10
- My idea is big enough to carry an entire story
  1 2 3 4 5 6 7 8 9 10

Where to next?

Now that you've chosen an idea for your story, we'll move to developing a structure for that story. We'll talk about constructing a basic plot. We'll emphasize the importance of conflict and action. And we'll debate the pros and cons of outlining. Soon your story will begin to take shape!

3

Structure a story

In our last chapter, we explored a variety of ways to generate story ideas. Then you chose which idea you want to develop first. Now that you have an idea to work with, we'll move on to story structure. You might think of structure as your story's foundation: as the skeleton to which you will go on to attach moving muscles, a beating heart, emotions and a unique voice. Your story structure is the thing that holds together all your other story elements; without it, your story would cave in on itself.

In my experiences working with new writers, many of them have shared that their biggest challenge is in structuring a story. They might have in mind an intriguing character or a great book idea – but they're stymied about how to turn those things into a coherent, compelling narrative.

If this has been a challenge for you, then there's good news: you've been absorbing story structure your entire life. And those experiences will help you as you learn more about creating a story structure for your children's story as well.

Key idea

Every time you heard a bedtime story, read a novel, or learned about something 'based on a true story', you were examining possible narrative structures. Every time you shared an anecdote at a social gathering or the family dinner table, you were rehearsing the best way to make a story sing for a listener.

Once upon a time...

If you find yourself struggling with structuring a story, one way to solve your problem is to retell a story already told by someone else. There is a theory that there are only a limited number of core stories in existence, so, to some degree, every writer is retelling a story already known to the audience. The key is to tell that story in such a way that readers feel like they are hearing it for the first time.

Of course, you cannot simply change a few words and call a story your own; at best, that's lazy writing and, at worst, it's copyright violation. However, you can take an existing plot – the sequence of events that make up a story – and rework it to such a degree that you make the story your own. This kind of retelling has proven popular in children's literature. Notable retellings range from *The True Story of the Three Little Pigs*, a picture book by author/ illustrator duo Jon Scieszka and Lane Smith that tells the story from the wolf's point of view, to Malinda Lo's *Ash*, a GLBT retelling of Cinderella for young adult readers.

Here are simple descriptions of four well-known fairy tales. Choose one of these storylines and rewrite it using a contemporary, realistic setting. Work to make the story your own, despite pulling from the basic plot of the original story – your goal is for readers to be able to recognize your original inspiration, but to feel that you have shed new light on or presented a unique twist to a timeworn tale. (And if you don't recognize the inspiration stories, I've listed those at the end of this chapter.)

Fairy Tale #1: A young brother and sister are separated from their poverty-stricken family. The lost children are enticed into the home of a predatory woman. Eventually, the children find a clever way to outwit their captor and escape with her wealth, and they are reunited with their father.

Fairy Tale #2: A complete misfit is born into a family of super-achievers. The child is initially ignored by family and ridiculed by peers. Ultimately, the child discovers a surprising truth about himself that leads him to a new family.

Fairy Tale #3: A stepmother is jealous of her stepdaughter's youth and beauty. Trouble escalates and the girl has to run away rather than risk harm from the stepmother. A group of misfits take her in and befriend her, but the stepmother continues to try to find the girl and harm her. Eventually, a rich young man falls in love with the girl, and through his help she is able to escape the stepmother for good.

Fairy Tale #4: Because of family circumstances, a beautiful young woman agrees to befriend a disfigured young man who is hidden away from regular life. The two develop a strong bond, yet the young woman is torn between the world she came from and the world of the young man, especially as she isn't sure she loves him as more than a friend. When it appears the young woman has abandoned him, the young man falls into a deep depression, and is only transformed by her eventual return and declaration of love.

Conflict is key

As we discuss different ways to structure a story, I urge you to keep one element in mind over all others: conflict, or the problem in your story. All of the familiar fairy tales in our exercise above had easily recognizable conflict. It might have taken the form of a failure to be accepted for whom one really is or a family dispute, but conflict is at the heart of each story. In fact, without conflict there is no story! And yet the lack of any conflict, or too little conflict, or conflict that is introduced too late or resolved too early or easily, are all recurring problems when I critique manuscripts by new writers.

Before you start plotting explosions and world wars, let me reassure you that your story's conflict doesn't have to measure as 'life-altering' on the Richter scale to be effective (although the popularity of dystopian novels proves that that level of conflict often makes for a great story). Here's an example. Eating one's vegetables might not be an earth-shattering dilemma, but, to a child character confronted by spinach, it can seem monumental. I have an editor friend who refers to this type of problem relativity as 'two inches of water'. In a worst-case scenario, you can drown in two inches of water. Everyone around you might be yelling, 'Just stand up and you'll be fine.' But you will still feel like you're drowning if the problem feels huge to you. Other people's opinion of the actual scale of trouble doesn't matter; even two inches of trouble seems too deep when it's a problem that is getting the best of you.

That's the effect you want to create for your reader: a sense that, for the character in question, the conflict (however small it might seem to someone else) represents a true crisis. You will usually work to build in the reader a sense of empathy for that character as he or she works through their crisis. And you will want to introduce the conflict very early in the story, so that the reader is hooked from the beginning. Today's readers have many distractions and other possible entertainments at hand – so, while old-fashioned children's stories might have started out in a more leisurely way, today's stories kick off with immediate conflict and action.

If you can clearly identify your story's conflict, you will find that structuring a story is much less difficult than you might have thought.

 Key idea

Conflict is key to a story, but conflict is in the eye of the character. If what is at stake feels huge to your main character, even if it seems trivial to others, then that qualifies as enough conflict on which to build a story.

Stir things up

At the end of the last chapter, you chose an idea that you wanted to tackle first as you continue to explore children's writing. Reframe that idea so that it contains a clear and specific conflict. For example, in the 'Harry Potter' series, there is a clear battle between good and evil, made most obvious in the conflict between Harry and Voldemort.

Putting together a plot

Key idea

All you need to know to begin plotting is the basic plot breakdown that writers have used since Aristotle's time: a good story must have a beginning, a middle and an end.

I earlier identified plot as the events that make up your story. Different writers have put forward different theories as to how many basic plot types exist (three or seven or even 36). Other writers have proposed various numbers of elements that make up a plot, or a variety of names for those elements. But, fortunately, getting started with plotting is much more straightforward than it might sound, if you focus on that triune of beginning/middle/end.

In the **beginning,** you'll likely start by trying to build a connection between your readers and a compelling character. Part of your job will be to hook those readers by quickly introducing a conflict that the character is trying to overcome. It should be the kind of problem that will resonate with the readers you have identified as your potential audience, the kind of struggle that will make children that age want to keep turning pages. Or, to frame it in a somewhat different way, you will introduce a character who has a relatable and urgent need or desire (a motivation, something at stake) – and then you will throw one or more obstacles in her path, the kind of obstacles that threaten her achievement of that goal.

In the story **middle,** you will have your character repeatedly attempt to overcome the problem or obstacle(s). Your job as a writer is to increase the sense of tension and suspense over the final outcome for readers. That means that you will likely choose to have the character make repeated attempts but fail each time. Each attempt will increase in intensity. In a dramatic story, each attempt and successive failure should feel more traumatic, edgier or dangerous; in a humorous story, the attempts and successive failures might be funnier, more over the top or more embarrassing for the character. Make your character take risks and suffer consequences; an overprotective writer is a boring writer.

For the end of your story, you will finally reach some sort of resolution. For younger readers – almost always for picture books, easy readers and chapter books – there will usually be a happy ending with a clear resolution. For older readers – sometimes for middle grade stories and more regularly in YA books – endings can be ambiguous or even dark.

Older readers can tolerate these more nuanced endings. But even then, writers often choose to provide, if not a happy ending, an ending that has a sense of hope for the character. For example, perhaps the character's deep desire – that his divorced parents will reunite – isn't realized. However, the ending leaves readers with a sense of reassurance that the character has now gained the tools he needs to survive his family crisis.

Along with the resolution to the conflict(s), you will also want to give readers a second type of ending: a sense of how the character has been transformed through facing the challenges and failures, and ultimately experiencing the resolution of her conflict. What did the character come to recognize about herself, or about how the world works? What will the character carry forward now that she has faced this particular challenge?

 Nolan Feeney, the *Atlantic*

'[T]here's almost always an underlying optimism in YA, an identifiable maturation or development that [young adult author Kathryn] Reiss calls "the kernel of hope." "There's a sense that it's worth waking up tomorrow," Reiss explains. "Things are dark, things are terrible, but tomorrow's another day. Ninety-nine percent of books for teens have that at least at the end."'

Linear or not?

A plot for the youngest readers will almost always be linear, moving forward from point A to point B and C in sequence and without flashbacks or side stories. Otherwise, these new readers will become quickly confused and overwhelmed by your story.

But a plot for a middle grade or YA novel does not have to be linear. You may choose to order your scenes in a way that builds suspense without following a sequence that is obvious (at least initially) to the reader.

Third time's the charm

Just as beginning/middle/end makes for a satisfying three-part plot, you can expand on the Rule of Three to map out a basic but workable storyline. Your simple outline will include basic descriptions for your idea, beginning, middle and end. The middle, however, will also be broken into three parts: First Attempt, Second Attempt, Third Attempt.

Jot a few notes for each of the steps below to create your basic story outline:

Idea: Write down the story idea you chose to move forward with in the last chapter.

Beginning: Based on your idea, select the story details you will need to know for your simple outline. As described above, this includes the basics about your main character (age, gender) and the core conflict he/she is confronting. You may or may not yet have decided these details for your official story, but that's fine. Make some quick choices for the purposes of this activity so you have elements to work with; you can definitely expand on or change them later.

Middle, First Attempt: Given the character and obstacle you have chosen, decide what your character might do for a first attempt to overcome that problem. Your character is most likely to try a fairly obvious solution, or something that draws on his preferences or strengths. For example, a character with a lot of personal charisma might try to charm his way around the problem; a character who is prone to rule-breaking might try a sneaky approach. For purposes of keeping the story going, this first attempt must fail!

Middle, Second Attempt: Your character has now failed to solve her problem. Think about how this makes you feel when this happens in real life: you are frustrated, disappointed, angry, discouraged. The problem likely seems even worse than you first realized; the stakes have been raised in terms of overcoming it. All of this is true for your character as well. For the second attempt to solve the problem, your character will likely choose to call on greater resources. Perhaps she will enlist allies, or try a more radical solution, or simply 'go bigger'. But again, to her enormous frustration, she will fail to solve the problem.

Middle, Third Attempt: Now the intensity level of your story has really ratcheted up. The stakes have risen to enormous proportions in the character's mind. This time when he tackles the problem, he will bring everything he has and then some to try to defeat the problem. He may have to enlist not only allies, but useful enemies. He may be forced to act in a way he didn't know he was capable of, such as a timid character who takes surprisingly bold action. He may choose to take an enormous personal risk.

End: The problem is somehow resolved. Depending on the age of the reader, there is either a clearly happy ending or, for an older reader, possibly a more nuanced ending – but still with some sort of resolution. Also, consider in what ways the character has been transformed by the repeated attempts and eventual success at resolving the problem. Has her life been changed in some way? Has he learned something critical about himself?

Do I have to outline?

The activity you just completed gives you a functional outline, a roadmap you could use to guide a story from beginning to end. So should this always be one of the first things you do when you set out to write a children's book?

Not necessarily. To outline, or not to outline: that is the question. Or at least one of the questions regularly debated by authors. Sometimes they even apply the terms 'plotter' and 'pantser' to the debate. Plotters carefully plan out the events of their story in advance of writing it. Pantsers do not outline in advance; instead, they follow their inspiration to see where the story leads them, writing 'by the seat of their pants'.

The debate between the two approaches is a regular feature of writing articles and online chat rooms for authors. There are strong advocates for both camps who can readily cite the pros and cons for the two sides. Plotters say an outline helps them write more efficiently and keeps them going on those days they don't feel particularly inspired. Pantsers love the sense of discovery that comes with letting the story take them where it will, and say it keeps their writing from becoming predictable.

Focus point

As with so many pieces of writing advice, the real answer in regards to whether you should outline or not is to use the approach that helps you make the steadiest continued progress on your work. If you find yourself stalling out, it may be time to switch tactics, or to try a hybrid approach that uses some of the tricks of both the plotters and the pantsers.

Which camp are you?

Are you a plotter or a pantser? You may find a few clues in how you operate in other arenas. Choose your preferred answer to each of the following questions:

1 When going on a trip, which of the following do you do?

   a   Plan out the entire trip in advance, researching which highlights to visit, making hotel reservations and checking travel guides for restaurant choices ☐

   b   Head out with a general sense of your ultimate destination, but avoid scheduling specific stops so that you can follow intriguing signs or the advice of friendly locals ☐

2   When cooking, which of the following are you more likely
     to do?
     a   Plan your menu in advance, make a shopping list,
          and follow an established recipe   ☐
     b   Buy whatever looks appealing and then throw it
          together, often testing new combinations   ☐
3   When putting together a new desk that arrived
     disassembled, which of the following do you do?
     a   Carefully read and then follow the instructions   ☐
     b   Look at the picture on the box and then follow
          your intuition   ☐

It's probably obvious that those with more 'a' answers might be
plotters, while the 'b' answers might signal pantsers. However
you tested, be open to both tactics: sometimes a hybrid approach
is best, or you may find that different projects require different
approaches.

Circling around

I've tested different outlining approaches with different writing
projects myself. Sometimes I write up a chapter-by-chapter plan
before I begin writing, and other times I draft without an outline to
see what structure appears as the story unfolds. Both have proven
effective at different times for me. My own key to success seems to
depend not as much on whether I outline or not, but on figuring out
the end of the story early in the process.

When I determine my ending in an early stage of planning my story,
I may have only a general sense of the overall resolution and the
character's transformation. Or I may have a very clear image in my
head of the final scene. I don't need to know every last detail of the
ending, but I do need to develop a strong sense of the emotional
resonance I want to leave in the mind of the reader as they close the
book and set it down a final time.

However detailed is my understanding of my story's ending, knowing
it early in the writing process has proven invaluable to me. But how
do you determine your story's ending if you haven't yet plotted out
the events leading up to it? By carefully considering your story's

beginning. You will introduce your conflict early in your story – so at the end, you must clearly show readers the impact of the resolution of that original conflict, or the series of conflicts it led to.

It is as if you are asking a question in the first sentence, paragraph or chapter (depending on the overall length of what you're writing), and then answering that same question at the end. Your answer can be surprising or unexpected, but it should feel as if it emerges inevitably from the story you've crafted (and the question it originally posed for readers). If you answer a different question than the one originally posed, your readers will feel confused or dissatisfied, as if they have lost their way in the story. A carefully plotted story works like the series of breadcrumbs that guide your readers to that final, inexorable answer. So having that ending in mind will guide your writing like a single beam of light on a dark night, whether you outline or not.

Then, by reading through to the end of the story, readers earn the right to the secret decoder ring that reveals the story secrets that were hinted at way back in the story beginning. The ending circles back to the beginning like a snake biting its own tail. Some stories, in fact, end in the same way that they began. S.E. Hinton's *The Outsiders*, sometimes credited as the original YA book, has the same opening and closing paragraph. But it is only by having read the entire story that readers truly understand all that paragraph has to offer.

Distinguished children's writer Richard Peck

'[T]he first chapter is the last chapter in disguise.'

A hybrid approach

So what would a hybrid approach to outlining look like? Here's a real-world example from my experience writing my middle grade mystery *Turn Left at the Cow*. I began with a strong opening image in mind, and a fairly good grasp of my character's urgent desire and the conflicts he was initially facing. But, shortly into writing the story, I then turned to figuring out the ending, exploring how the overall conflict might be finally resolved, and where I needed my character to be emotionally as the story drew to a close.

With that clear sense of both the beginning and ending of the story, I then set out through the barren landscape of the middle without first creating an outline. I knew that for a mystery, both surprise elements and careful plotting are necessary. But I wanted to allow for the sense of discovery and unanticipated developments that writing without an outline might afford me. So I kept asking myself, 'What happens next?' – always pushing for unexpected developments that would still make logical sense to my readers, and I managed to make steady forward progress.

The problem came at a certain point about three-quarters of the way through, where my writing completely floundered. I had too many open-ended possibilities, and not enough word count left to include them all. I needed to somehow funnel my story down to fit into the ending I already knew the story needed.

So at that point I stopped writing and created an outline in reverse! Starting with my known ending, I asked myself what needed to happen in the scene immediately before that to set up that ending scene. Then I asked myself what had to happen before that, to set up that scene. In that way, I worked backwards to where I had stalled out – but I now had an outline that effectively took me all the way to the end of my story. I picked up where I had left off, and began writing forward again.

What should you write first?

 Focus point

Even if your plot is linear, you may choose to tackle the writing of your work in a non-linear fashion. Sometimes the best way to make progress is to write, not what you think will become the next scene in your story, but the scene that is screaming loudest for your attention at the moment you sit down to write.

Some writers begin writing at the beginning of the story and move forward sequentially all the way to the ending. Others follow their writing energy and jump around, writing the scene that captures their attention that day and then reordering the scenes they've written later in the revision process. If you are a new writer, I would suggest that you begin with the beginning and keep going from there as far as you can. If you get stuck, try switching to a scene that has great writing energy for you to see whether that approach works better.

Action is key

Just as conflict in a story doesn't have to include warfare or explosions, action can also be more nuanced. Dialogue – a discussion or debate between characters – can count as action. A character making a key emotional realization can count as action. But something must be happening that actively engages the reader. And the action shouldn't just be random; it should be tied to forwarding the plot.

You want to include action all throughout your story. Hook readers with something attention-grabbing right from the start, something that makes them sit up and take notice. Action works beautifully as this kind of hook. Again, while old-fashioned children's books might have allowed for more leisurely beginnings and a longer set-up, today's stories demand that you throw readers right into action and conflict. Writers often feel compelled to tell readers all of the back story that led the character up to that moment of acting or being acted upon. But the truth is, readers will go along for the ride if they are swept up in the excitement of an active opening scene. They'll have the patience to wait for all of their questions to be answered if there's enough happening to keep them invested in your story. But if they're bored by too many long explanations and inaction, they'll slam shut the covers of your book and move on to another source of entertainment.

David LaRochelle, the opening to the picture book *The Best Pet of All*

'On Monday I asked my mother if I could have a dog.
'"A dog is a good pet," I said.
'"No," she said.'

 Maggie Stiefvater, the opening to the young adult novel *The Scorpio Races*

'It is the first day of November and so, today, someone will die.'

 Hook your reader

The two key quotes referenced here are story openings – one for a picture book and one for a young adult novel. In just a few words, each author hooks readers with drama and conflict.

For this activity, I'm going to have you do a writing exercise based on one suggested by mystery writer Ellen Hart when I took one of her classes. It totally changed the direction of my story and could do the same for you! Here it is. Write three completely different opening paragraphs for your story. The different openings should all be based on the same story concept, but experiment to come up with three very different approaches to kicking off your story's action. Try different means of hooking your reader. When you are done, read over each of them. Which opening reads the strongest to you?

Keep it moving

Moving on from your active beginning, every subsequent scene should include some clear action. The action will likely be tied to the conflict in some way. By continuing to incorporate action and build the conflict throughout your story, you will add the kind of tension and suspense that will keep young readers turning pages. The action will likely escalate as the story moves forward and you raise the stakes for your character.

In a picture book, that means that every spread (the two facing pages of the book) should show some new action: a physical event, a change of locations, a new character entering, a conversation, new information revealed to readers.

In a longer work, every chapter should have one or more active scenes. Even in a story for older readers that is unlikely to be illustrated, you should be able to clearly picture something happening in the story, as if it was being portrayed on a movie screen.

Key idea

A critical aspect to creating a satisfying ending will be to have your young character take direct action of some kind to solve her problem for herself. Certainly an adult (parent, teacher, coach) can give advice. But allowing the grown-ups to fix everything is too much like real life; child readers crave a world where young people are smart enough and strong enough to solve their own problems. Make your young character act in some bold fashion to resolve her conflict.

Build your story scene by scene

A scene is a sequence of continuous action. Thinking about your story as a series of scenes, much like it would appear if turned into a movie, can be enormously helpful. It allows you to identify if you are including enough action. It illuminates where there are gaps. It shows you whether your storyline is holding together in a way that will make sense for your readers.

Even many picture books, as short as they are, have multiple scenes. It can be difficult to come up with enough potential variety for an illustrator if you stick exclusively to the same setting without a break in time, which is what is required for a scene. So another way to outline your story is to break it down by scenes. Even if you aren't writing by outline, it can be helpful to think in terms of 'scene by scene': as you finish one scene, think through the basics of the next one you are going to work on.

Scene screen

Return to the outline you created in the 'Third time's the charm' activity. Further break down your outline by detailing the first scene of your story. You don't have to provide an enormous amount of detail, but try to provide the following information:

- The place and time of the scene
- The characters in the scene
- The key actions in the scene

Then if you are able, move on to detail other scenes in your story.

As an example, here's a detailing of the first scene from my book *Turn Left at the Cow*:

Setting:

Grandmother's creepy cellar

Characters:

main character Trav (13)

neighbour Kenny (13), whom Trav is meeting for the first time

Kenny's cousin Iz (13), whom Trav is meeting for the first time

Trav's father is key to the action but doesn't appear; he died before Trav was born

Key actions:

Trav falls into the cellar freezer chest on to what he thinks is a frozen human head

Trav meets Kenny and Iz, who explain the origins of the head to him

Iz tells Trav the shocking news that his father was a bank robber, and that she and Kenny are searching for the bank loot, believed to be hidden nearby

Workshop

1 Review

For the 'Third time's the charm' activity, you created an outline for a potential story. Considering all that you have learned so far, rate your outline on the following (1 being the lowest score, 10 being the highest):

- My outline sets up an engaging story beginning.
  1 2 3 4 5 6 7 8 9 10

- My outline sets up a suspenseful story middle.
  1 2 3 4 5 6 7 8 9 10

- My outline sets up a satisfying story ending.
  1 2 3 4 5 6 7 8 9 10

- My overall outline sets up a workable story.
  1 2 3 4 5 6 7 8 9 10

2 Close-up

My outline sets up an engaging story beginning

- Does the beginning grab the reader's attention?
- Is the conflict introduced early in the story – within the first few lines of a picture book or early reader, or the first few pages of a longer book?
- Is the main character's desire or need apparent?

Bearing in mind your response to the questions above, what could you add or change in your outline that will more likely lead to an engaging story? Modify the beginning of your outline.

My outline sets up a suspenseful story middle

- Does the character confront, and fail to defeat, at least two obstacles?
- Is there an escalating sense of what's at stake, leading to a heightened sense of suspense?
- Does your character ultimately risk something important?

Bearing in mind your response to the questions above, what could you add or change in your outline that will more likely lead to a suspenseful story? Modify the middle portions of your outline.

My outline sets up a satisfying story ending

- Does the main character ultimately solve the problem for him/herself?
- Does the ending answer the question asked in the beginning?
- Does the ending provide both some kind of resolution to the conflict and a sense of the emotional transformation of the character?

Bearing in mind your response to the questions above, what could you add or change in your outline that will more likely lead to a satisfying story? Modify the end of your outline.

My overall outline sets up a workable story

- Is there a variety of scenes within your story?
- Is there new action (physical or emotional) for each spread of a picture book, or each scene or chapter of an older reader's book?
- Is the plot simple enough for the targeted audience (if I have one in mind) to follow?

Bearing in mind your response to the questions above, what could you add or change in your outline that will more likely lead to a workable story? Modify your outline.

3 Re-review

Now read your revised work and re-rate the following from 1 to 10:

- My outline sets up an engaging story beginning.

  1 2 3 4 5 6 7 8 9 10

- My outline sets up a suspenseful story middle.

  1 2 3 4 5 6 7 8 9 10

- My outline sets up a satisfying story ending.

  1 2 3 4 5 6 7 8 9 10

- My overall outline sets up a workable story.

  1 2 3 4 5 6 7 8 9 10

Where to next?

Now that you've started to structure your story, and come up with an opening paragraph, we'll move to peopling that story with relatable characters. We'll also talk about writing dialogue that gives those characters a voice, and choosing a point of view that most effectively conveys the story to your readers.

In case you didn't recognize them, here are the source stories for the 'Once upon a time' activity:
- 'Hansel and Gretel'
- 'The Ugly Duckling'
- 'Snow White'
- 'Beauty and the Beast'

4

Breathe life into characters

For many writers, there is no more important element of a story than the main character. Your main character is the central figure in your story; he or she is the person or creature that makes things happen, and that things happen to. Your main character will become the beating heart of the entire book, the emotional core of the story. It is through that character that many a writer has found their way into the story that demands to be heard – and on the other end of the writing equation, the main character is often the element that fully engages young readers in that same story.

Creating a compelling, relatable character is critical. In this chapter, we'll examine some of the ways that you can make your characters spring to life in your own head, so that you can then go on to make them spring to life for your readers.

Connect to the conflict

In the last chapter we focused on structuring a story that would keep readers turning pages. A key to creating suspense in your writing is that you must at all costs avoid acting as an overprotective parent to your characters: you must throw them into the deep end at every turn. Your story will lack the necessary conflict unless you risk your character's happiness – and, in some cases, even your character's life! Heap trouble upon your main character's head; make him sweat to earn the satisfying resolution to his story.

In the end, character and plot are inextricably linked. The conflict emerges because of a character who is struggling with some problem, or who is facing down the obstacles that stand between her achievement of some urgent need or desire. Remember the two inches of water from Chapter 3? The conflict will seem particularly monumental because of the character you choose; to another character, that particular problem might not be so daunting. Make sure that your combination of character and conflict seem like an organic, natural pairing – it's like matchmaking the right character with the right problem.

Don't forget your target audience

 Key idea

Your target audience is an important consideration when developing your character. Young people often prefer to read about a character who is their own age or a little bit older.

Most children relate more easily to the problems and concerns of other children near their own age. They are also excited about the notion of 'getting bigger' and experiencing the greater independence and excitement offered by the next stage of life. They mimic older children's fashions and covet their entertainment choices. A six-year-old won't necessarily be able to connect to the concerns of a 13-year-old, but they will definitely be intrigued by the intoxicating possibilities offered by turning seven or eight.

Who do you think they are?

At this point you've identified a core idea and a basic plot that includes a character confronting a problem. You may already know several things about your character. If you are still debating between different character possibilities, now is the time to choose which main character you want to work with for your first story.

Start a list of any and all details that you think apply to your main character: gender, age, personality, family, friends, where they live, what they enjoy doing. You may have a sense of their deepest heart's desire. Write down everything you already know, big or small.

You will want to keep a fact sheet such as this for every character you create for your story. Whenever you assign a detail to him or her – a birthday, a middle name, a favourite food – add it to this fact sheet. It will save you much time down the road.

'Real' and relatable

Key idea

For a children's book, your main character will almost always be a child or teenager rather than an adult.

Children are much more engaged when sharing the perspective of another child; they are not yet absorbed by the adult world and its concerns. It's not that you can't tell a story about a beloved grandparent in a children's book. But you will almost always choose to tell that story from the perspective of the grandchild as the main character, rather than the grandparent.

Of course, you will find many a non-human character in children's books as well: sparkly vampires and sexy angels for the older set; rambunctious bears and naughty bunnies for the younger set. Despite their other-than-human status, one of the key ingredients for stirring up a compelling character is someone who is highly relatable and shares the same real struggles and dreams as your human audience.

Sometimes a dog in a children's book is just a dog. But often, animals in a children's story are meant to be stand-ins for human children – what people in the children's book world sometimes call 'kids with fur'. Sometimes it's an author's way of tackling divisive issues such as racism – it's easier to talk about differences when it's the cat family and the dog family having a dispute. Sometimes it's a way to provide more freedom to a child in the story – it's much more likely that Little Rabbit would be walking through the woods alone than a human toddler. And sometimes it's just a creative choice on the part of the author or illustrator to make the story more fun.

At any rate, when you do include kids with fur in your story, the trick is to make them highly relatable to your young readers. Peter Rabbit is much like any other naughty little boy. The Little Engine That Could (neither human nor animal) is relatable because he is the littlest engine in a world of bigger engines, a problem any small child can connect with. The rat in your story might have some rat-like characteristics, but if he's a kid with fur, he will also have a human side that allows a child to engage with him.

Likewise in YA, teenage werewolves or vampires – while living with their particular supernaturally cursed states – will suffer the same problems and obstacles that confront their human teenage counterparts: the upheaval of first love, not fitting in with their peers, family turmoil. Even in stories set in dystopian worlds, which on the surface seem the definition of 'unreal', the characters are led by the need to save a world that adults have set on a course for disaster. What better description could there be for actual teenagers who feel that the adults around them have messed up the world they will inherit?

 Key idea

Give your characters the characteristics and age-specific conflicts that will resonate with your target audience, making those characters seem real and authentic even if they are talking skunks or lovesick zombies.

Time capsule

The items a person values say a lot about him. What a child carries in his pocket or her backpack, hides in his closet or stores in her car, might all provide telling clues as to who they are.

For this writing activity, you are going to create a time capsule for your character. Typically, someone would create a time capsule for an important new building; they would gather objects that reflect the particular time, place and lifestyle of the people responsible for the building.

Select 20 objects that likewise reveal something important about your character. These might include: family photographs, sports trophies, T-shirts from favourite vacation spots, favourite books, artworks, scouting badges, journals, favourite toys, keepsakes, jewellery, favourite movies or music, technology items, etc. You don't have to explain why you are including every item, but be specific. Don't just say 'her favourite book'; list the title of the actual book.

You have permission to break two of the laws of science: you have the ability to shrink a large object down to fit into your virtual time capsule, and you can preserve a favourite food item so that it doesn't spoil. Don't include any live creatures, however; instead, include something to represent them: a dog collar, a cat toy, a photograph.

If you are a very visual person, you might enjoy finding pictures and putting them together to create a visual representation of your character's time capsule.

Then choose one item off your list and explain in further detail how it represents something critical about your character. Here is a real-life example. I have nephews who are identical twins. From the time they were two years old, every morning one of them would use a massive amount of hair product so that his hair stuck straight up. Once when he came to visit me overnight, he brought only a stuffed animal, a clean pair of underpants and enough hair gel to style my entire neighbourhood.

For years we tried to figure out this obsession of his – did he want to become a hairstylist? Was he vain? And then, one day, one of my friends got him to explain.

'This is my own personal hair!' he said. 'When I do this, nobody calls me my by brother's name.'

For him, the hair product represented much more than what appeared on the surface: it was an expression of his search for personal identity and his desire to be seen as an individual separate from his identical twin.

Choose one of the items off your character's list and write a similar explanation of that item's deeper meaning.

Pleased to meet you

Your main character is one of your strongest entry points for your readers; it is the element that will make them feel emotionally connected to your story. If they connect with your character, they will likely continue to turn pages, to see whether that character somehow manages to overcome the problems she's confronting.

But be sure to create a main character who is compelling but not perfect! Nobody is more boring, or feels less authentic, than a character who never makes mistakes. Make your character flawed in a way that readers will find believable and understandable.

You will also want to make your main character charismatic or engaging. Is this someone whom young readers will want to spend time with? That doesn't mean that your character has to be completely likable. But if your character has hard edges that might put off readers, look to find a way to reveal some vulnerability, some way for those readers to feel a sense of empathy for that character. It is all about building that connection between the character and readers.

Appropriate behaviour

One of the most common character-related problems I find when I critique manuscripts-in-progress is that the writer is giving conflicting cues about the character's age. Be careful to make sure that you have a specific age in mind for your character. Then, make sure that every behaviour, the way they think and speak and act, the way they process the world, are all consistent with a child that age. In Chapter 2, we discussed how you might gain a basic understanding of the stages of child development. This is another time when those resources will come in very handy.

Beyond the question of age-level cues, you will also want to ask yourself whether your character is acting 'in character'. Do the actions you have them taking represent the actions someone of that emotional make-up is likely to take? How would the character you have portrayed likely respond to the stress of a big problem? Do that character's particular actions and ways of behaving drive the plot? To make a character feel authentic, they can only act in the way a person with those characteristics would act, when met with the complications of your plot.

Reflect on the activities we did in Chapter 1, when you consciously tried to return to the emotional reality of being a child or teenager. Children and teens are quite discerning readers; they will reject a story that feels inauthentic or that seems to portray a childhood or adolescent experience that seems fake or has been superimposed upon by adult nostalgia or the desire to teach them a lesson.

Acting out

Consider what you know about your character's emotional make-up, personality, age, gender and family training. Then work your way down the list below, describing briefly how he or she would react when experiencing the following emotions. Would they talk to someone or keep their feelings a secret? What would they say? How would they respond physically?

- Rage
- Disappointment
- Grief
- Jubilation

- Hilarity
- Embarrassment
- Desire for revenge

Supporting characters

You will want your supporting characters to feel believable and authentic as well. Their role in the story is likely connected to providing a backdrop for your character, or as an ally or adversary in the conflict.

But avoid the danger of assuming that because a character is playing a supporting role, it's OK for you to fall back on a character stereotype when portraying her. Teenage 'mean girls' really do exist. But simply inserting the stereotype into your story will make it seem stale and predictable. If the mean girl is important to the story, find a way to catch readers' attention by turning her into a fully fleshed-out human being, one who has vulnerabilities.

Another danger is in allowing the adults in the story to take over. Children know all too well that adults hold most of the power in the world; when they read, they crave stories where young people are empowered. There's a reason there are so many famous orphans in children's books! It's not that children want their parents to die. It's that they enjoy living vicariously through people their own age who have to make their own way in the world, who must survive without adults fixing everything that goes wrong. In actuality, nothing much interesting (as far as trouble goes) is allowed to happen if there's an adult firmly in charge. Books allow for all sorts of interesting trouble to develop.

 Focus point

If you find that your story feels overly safe or that your character is sitting back and allowing grown-ups to fix everything, then push the adults to the back of your story – or get rid of them altogether. Return the attention, and the power, to your young character.

Let's talk

Dialogue is a conversation between two or more characters. It's a key part of most stories. As we discussed in Chapter 3, it's also a form of action; whether your characters are arguing, exchanging loving whispers, or begging for assistance, they are taking action of some kind. Therefore dialogue is an excellent way to move your plot forward. It can also be a handy device for filling in readers on back-story details; rather than long paragraphs where a character muses over how they reached a certain point, you can have one character explaining to another what has gone before. However, avoid having one character tell another character something they clearly already know; this will ring false to your readers.

Dialogue also adds to your story's credibility. And it is an easy way to create the effect of an easy-to-read page for young readers; every time there is a new speaker you indent, creating an inviting look to your story. Strive to create a pleasing balance between dialogue and narrative text.

One of dialogue's greatest features is that it allows you to illuminate your characters. Each character's voice – what he says (or doesn't say) and how he says it – provides key clues to who each character is as a person. Each of your characters should sound distinct. Their voices will reflect things such as their age, life experience, education, geographic location, personality. A grandfather and his grandson will likely speak quite differently because they are from different generations, but even two children who are the same age will have subtle differences in their speech.

MAKING DIALOGUE READABLE

Writing dialogue can be tricky. Writers can become self-conscious about all of the functions they are trying to serve; it can lose the spontaneous feel of real speech. On the other hand, if you try to produce an exact recreation of how people speak, you will discover that it makes for tedious reading. Listening to children or teens can help you enormously in terms of capturing the nuances of how they talk. Eavesdrop at the mall, coffee shops or library story hours. But you want to recreate these eavesdropping sessions artfully rather than directly.

Be especially wary with current slang. It can quickly sound dated and will irk readers. Try to judge whether a slang term has a chance of enduring beyond the next six months, and then use it very sparingly.

On the other hand, dialogue that is written in an overly formal way is equally unworkable. It will come off as stilted and unreal. Voice will trump grammar every time if your characters are to come off as real. Find a balancing point between formal English and actual speech.

Here are a few keys to creating dialogue:

- People almost always use contractions when speaking ('I'm' instead of 'I am').
- People pause, repeat themselves, let their thoughts trail off, and speak in incomplete phrases. Don't overdo when including these devices, but incorporate some of them to make your dialogue more believable.
- Speakers often interrupt each other.
- It's tempting to have characters continuously call each other by name, but in real life people don't tend to do this as often as we think. People also tend to use pet names for each other ('Honey', 'Stupid', 'Baby').
- Wrap some action into the dialogue for variety and a sense of authenticity.

DIALOGUE TAGS

Your characters' voices should sound so uniquely 'them' that an experienced reader could likely identify the speaker even without attribution, or dialogue tags (such as 'he said').

When writing for children, however, you will likely include more dialogue tags than when writing for adults. Since children are less experienced readers, they need the aid to interpreting who is speaking. The younger your reader, the more necessary the tags.

Some writers work to find different substitutes for 'said'. However, for the most part you will want to stick with 'said'. Save your 'whispered', 'shouted' and 'stammered' for very occasional use, and the fact that you have used something different will stand out and have a strong impact on readers.

Avoid using a word that is not actually a way of talking; for example, don't say something like: '"Of course you did," Mary giggled.' You can't speak while giggling, so you wouldn't use 'giggled' in a tag.

There is a way, however, to eliminate some of the omnipresent use of 'said'. If you have a character take an action immediately before or after a line of dialogue, the reader will assume that the character is the one speaking. Here are some examples of how this works:

'Of course you did.' Mary giggled. [In this case, Mary giggles after she finishes speaking, indicated by the period after 'did' – so this use is fine. The reader will assume that Mary is the speaker because they will link together the dialogue and the subsequent action Mary takes.]

'I just can't do it!' John pounded his fist on the table. [The reader will assume John is the speaker.]

Susie twirled around so that her skirt billowed like sails. 'I can't wait to see Owen!' [The reader will assume Susie is the speaker.]

Look who's talking

The best way to practise dialogue and to begin to hear your characters is to set them to talking. For this activity, your main character will discuss the conflict they are facing at the beginning of your story by having three different conversations with three different people (a parent, a coach, a friend, a romantic interest, an enemy, an aunt, a social worker, etc.). If you don't anticipate having many characters in your story, invent some additional characters for this exercise.

This will allow you to develop the voices of these different characters and explore the conflict from the main character's perspective. But also keep in mind the relationships in place, and how that will affect exactly what your main character will share with each individual. For example, a teenager might share something with a best friend that they would never tell a parent. Or a child might lie about a family secret to a teacher. Each of your three conversations should sound different based on the conversants.

When you are finished, read the three conversations out loud so you can hear your dialogue.

 Focus point

It is important to read your work out loud. You will hear it completely differently than when you read in your head, and you will catch areas where the writing sounds awkward. Remember that children's books are often read out loud! Reading out loud is especially important when writing dialogue.

Pondering point of view

Over time I've worked with hundreds of new writers, and I think that the craft area that gives them more trouble than any other is managing point of view. Basically, choosing a point of view involves choosing who is going to narrate the story. Some writers struggle with determining which point of view to use. Many more struggle with managing the point of view they choose, often without recognizing that they are tripping themselves up.

As with so many other choices you will make as a writer, your goal with point of view is to relay your story in the most effective way possible. Your point of view choice can also serve to invite readers inside your story – to make them feel that they are a part of what is happening on the page.

Because point of view is tricky, my best advice as you get started is to stick to one of the two point of view choices I'm going to outline here. They have both proven to be especially effective when writing for children. And you will have run across them time and again in your own reading – and will therefore find them familiar.

Key idea

Once you have a little more practice under your belt, you can move on to other point-of-view options. But to begin, you may want to choose between first person and third person limited to avoid some of the point-of-view pitfalls that new writers so easily fall into.

FIRST PERSON

Suzanne Collins, *The Hunger Games* (first-person point of view)

'A boy, I think from District 9, reaches the pack at the same time I do and for a brief time we grapple for it and then he coughs, splattering my face with blood. I stagger back, repulsed by the warm, sticky spray. Then the boy slips to the ground. That's when I see the knife in his back.'

First-person point of view is when the writer uses the 'I' voice. In this point of view, readers follow along as the viewpoint character shares his or her personal version of their experiences. Readers can know only what the character knows and experience only what the character experiences. If the viewpoint character falls asleep, is knocked unconscious or leaves the room, the action stops.

The character acts as a filter for readers. If your narrator is a teenage boy whom you've shown to be driven by hormones and cars, he will likely notice the make and model of the vehicles he passes, but is highly unlikely to notice the colour of an old woman's coat – she isn't in his field of interest. His knowledge and attitudes will shape what he focuses on, and therefore what he shares with the reader. His observations may be unreliable – perhaps his father isn't really the monster he portrays – but the reader will have to discern that from the father's actions and not from the son's reports.

In first person, the voice of the character is paramount. When using this point of view, writers must work to make sure that their character sounds like him- or herself (a young person with limited experience), and not like the writer (an adult with broader experience in the world). This leads to one of the complications of this point of view: it is difficult to effectively capture an authentic-sounding first-person voice for a young child. Young children have limited vocabularies and writing skills, and limited knowledge. To write in a five-year-old first-person voice that is both inviting and authentic can be a huge challenge, and sometimes leads to an unworkable story. Therefore, first person is used much less often in books for the youngest readers.

But first person is an extremely popular choice for young adult books, and is also featured in some middle grade books. It creates a feeling of intensity and builds a strong empathetic connection between readers and the character. Teenage and almost-teen readers love the deep immersion in story that the choice of first person offers. If this is your target audience, you will want to seriously consider using first-person point of view.

THIRD PERSON LIMITED

J.K. Rowling, *Harry Potter and the Philosopher's / Sorcerer's Stone* (third-person limited point of view)

'*Then a pain like he'd never felt before pierced his head; it was as though his scar were on fire. Half blinded, he staggered backward. He heard hooves behind him, galloping, and something jumped clean over Harry, charging at the figure.*'

Third-person point of view is when there is an outside narrator who refers to characters as 'he', 'she' or 'them'. There are different options for third person. For example, third person omniscient is an all-knowing voice that can dip into the heads of all of the characters in the story (a choice that also tends to distance readers). In third person limited, by contrast, the narrator is limited to knowing the internal thoughts and emotions of only one character, which tends to build a connection between readers and that character.

In the 'Harry Potter' series, we experience most of the story as if we are inside Harry's head, sharing in what happens to him and how it makes him feel (but different from first person since Harry is not himself the narrator). Just as in first person, however, we are limited to the things that Harry knows and experiences; in third person limited, it is off limits for the narrator to dip inside the heads of other characters. When Rowling needs the reader to have information that Harry isn't privy to, she often creates clever magical devices that give him access to that knowledge.

Third person limited is an extremely common choice for all fiction, and therefore usually feels comfortable for new writers: you have been hearing this narrative voice all of your reading life. Its other great advantage is that like first person, it puts readers inside the action of the story. However, because the narrator is not that main character, you are not limited by the vocabulary and knowledge base of your main character in the way you are with first person. Your outside narrator can convey the story in a way that a five-year-old first-person narrator couldn't.

When you are writing picture books, easy readers, chapter books, and the younger range of middle grade books, third person limited will most often be your preferable point of view choice. It is an option for YA writers as well.

WRITING WITH MULTIPLE VIEWPOINT CHARACTERS

Sometimes books for older readers include multiple viewpoint characters. These writers aren't using third person omniscient; instead, after a clear switch from one section to another, they relay the story through a different viewpoint character (instead of being able to dip into all the characters' consciousness simultaneously). Within the first section, the writer will stick strictly with the initial viewpoint character (either in first person or third person limited). Then, in the new section, the writer will stick strictly with the second viewpoint character. After another clear break, the story might switch viewpoint character again.

One purpose in taking this approach is to highlight a relationship. In the 'Sisterhood of the Traveling Pants' series, Ann Brashares rotates between her viewpoint characters from chapter to chapter, viewing the girls' friendship through multiple lenses. In Wendelin Van Draanen's *Flipped*, a boy and girl describe their relationship in alternating chapters, so that readers gain a sense of the truth of what happens between them through their contrasting viewpoints.

This approach can be effective for older readers, but would prove too confusing for most younger readers. And it doesn't give writers permission to 'head-hop'. That's the term applied when a writer jumps from the inside of one character's head to another within the same section of text, without a clearly marked break. New writers often make this mistake, especially when they want the reader to have a piece of information their viewpoint character doesn't yet have.

 ## Focus point

Remember to stay within the perspective of your viewpoint character. Otherwise you risk confusing readers and distancing them from your character. As you write, check yourself periodically to see whether you are still firmly 'inside' the viewpoint character for that section of the story.

 ## Differing views

Write a scene that features someone being tormented. It could be a scene that might figure into your story or something completely separate. It might be a young person being picked on by a bully, or a battle between siblings, or a hazing ritual. First write the scene from the perspective of the character who is being victimized. Stay completely inside that character's viewpoint as you tell the story.

Then tell the story again, except this time switch to the tormentor's viewpoint. Relate the same events, but this time stay completely within the tormentor's perspective as you tell the story.

Consider your two pieces. What did you learn about point of view by limiting yourself to one viewpoint in each case? Did you learn anything surprising about the tormentor by exploring the story from his or her perspective?

Getting inside the character

All of the elements we explored in this chapter offer opportunities to put readers inside the experiences and emotions of your character. The more you know about your character, even if it doesn't directly appear in your story, the more likely that your character will feel real and relatable to readers. Eventually, your character will seem so real to you that you might have to remind yourself that he or she is not a child you might bump into on the street!

For this activity, you are going to interview your character – asking the character a series of questions, and answering them on the character's behalf – two different times. Interview them first right before the action of your story begins, when they are just contemplating the need to tackle the story's conflict.

Then interview them again, but this time after what you project to be the endpoint of your story, after the conflict has been resolved. Remember, your character will somehow change or transform because of the experiences of your story, and their answers should reveal something of that transformation.

Here is a list of questions to get you started. But you don't need to use all of these questions, and can of course add several of your own, depending on what will produce information that is most fruitful for you as a writer.

- What does your character most need or desire?
- What is your character's biggest secret?
- In what ways does your character sabotage him- or herself?
- What trait, quality or physical characteristic does your character most dislike about him- or herself?
- Does your character have some kind of a ritual or superstition they follow? What is it, and why does it matter to him/her?
- What is your character most afraid of?
- What or who makes your character most angry?
- What would your character find funny?
- How has your character's family influenced them?
- What is your character's favourite activity? Why?

After you've finished both sets of answers (before and after the story's action), write about your character's transformation from the beginning to the end of your story. How does your character experience the series of events that take place in your story? How does it change your character? This is also known as your character arc. If you are contemplating using first-person point of view, describe your character arc as if it were being written by your character. If you plan to use third person limited, write about the character arc in third person limited.

Workshop

1 Review

For the 'Getting inside the character' activity, you described your story's character arc. Considering all that you have learned so far, rate your description on the following (1 being the lowest score, 10 being the highest):

- My conflict and character are well matched.

  ⬚1⬚ ⬚2⬚ ⬚3⬚ ⬚4⬚ ⬚5⬚ ⬚6⬚ ⬚7⬚ ⬚8⬚ ⬚9⬚ ⬚10⬚

- My characters are believable.

  ⬚1⬚ ⬚2⬚ ⬚3⬚ ⬚4⬚ ⬚5⬚ ⬚6⬚ ⬚7⬚ ⬚8⬚ ⬚9⬚ ⬚10⬚

- My main character is relatable.

  ⬚1⬚ ⬚2⬚ ⬚3⬚ ⬚4⬚ ⬚5⬚ ⬚6⬚ ⬚7⬚ ⬚8⬚ ⬚9⬚ ⬚10⬚

- I have chosen an effective point of view.

  ⬚1⬚ ⬚2⬚ ⬚3⬚ ⬚4⬚ ⬚5⬚ ⬚6⬚ ⬚7⬚ ⬚8⬚ ⬚9⬚ ⬚10⬚

2 Close-up

My conflict and character are well matched

- Is this a conflict a child of the character's age could feasibly experience?
- Since my target audience will likely be the same age or slightly younger than my character, will the target audience be drawn into the conflict I've chosen?
- Based on who I know my character to be, will this feel like a true conflict to them (even if it might not to someone else)?

- Have I allowed my character to find the kind of trouble that will keep the story interesting, and empowered them to solve their own problem? (In other words, have I kept adults at the background of my story?)

Bearing in mind your response to the questions above, what could you change in your character or conflict that will more likely lead to a workable story? Modify the character arc accordingly.

My characters are believable

- Do I know my character well enough?
- Does my character feel like someone with a life and a history that happened before the story's beginning?
- Does my character have flaws and make mistakes?
- Does my character give age-appropriate cues to the reader?
- Are my supporting characters more than stereotypes?

Bearing in mind your response to the questions above, what could you add to your knowledge of, or change about, your characters? Modify the character arc accordingly.

My main character is relatable

- Is my main character a child or teenager?
- If not, is my main character an entity that has the qualities of a child or teenager?
- Does my main character share the kind of underlying struggles and dreams that my readers also experience?
- Have I given readers a reason to feel a sense of empathy or attachment for my character despite the character's flaws?

Bearing in mind your response to the questions above, what could you add to your knowledge of, or change about, your characters? Modify the character arc accordingly.

I have chosen an effective point of view

- Did I feel comfortable writing in this point of view?
- If I wrote in first person, does the voice sound like a child or teenager who is the age of my character?

- Did I stay within my viewpoint character's perspective, not bringing in information he or she didn't have?

Bearing in mind your response to the questions above, have you chosen the right point of view? If you struggled with the writing or feel like the point of view didn't work, try writing the character arc again, but this time using the alternate point of view we discussed in this chapter. Which point of view choice seems to work best for you in the end?

3 Re-review

Now read your revised work and re-rate the following from 1 to 10:

- My conflict and character are well matched.

  ① ② ③ ④ ⑤ ⑥ ⑦ ⑧ ⑨ ⑩

- My characters are believable.

  ① ② ③ ④ ⑤ ⑥ ⑦ ⑧ ⑨ ⑩

- My main character is relatable.

  ① ② ③ ④ ⑤ ⑥ ⑦ ⑧ ⑨ ⑩

- I have chosen an effective point of view.

  ① ② ③ ④ ⑤ ⑥ ⑦ ⑧ ⑨ ⑩

Where to next?

Now that you've started to bring your characters to life, you need to create a framework in which they can take action. In the next chapter we'll talk about building a world for your characters to inhabit, and describing it through the kind of sensory details that will make your readers feel as if they are experiencing it first-hand.

5

Build a world

Your setting is the place and the time of your story. It's another key tool that you can use to engage your readers. Through an apt depiction of your setting(s), you will lure readers to inhabit the world of your book alongside your characters, sharing their emotional journey through that world.

Your story may very likely have several settings, and the character may be moving from one setting to another, or through several settings, over the course of your story. There is the bigger world of your story (which may or may not be Earth or the present time). Your character will be located in a specific land within that bigger world. Within that land they might be connected to a specific community, and within that community, they will move between different environments: perhaps their school, a friend's house, an entertainment area, and their own home. And within their own home, there may be several key settings: the family gathering place, the character's bedroom and so on.

The time of your story may also change: from one time of day to another, from one season to another, from year to year, or from one season of life to another. In time travel stories, there are actual jumps in time!

Your key settings

Make a list of all of the settings you can think of that will make up your story, labelling them as both a place and with the time(s) they become a significant backdrop for the action. (If you are not yet sure about how much time passes in your story, you can approximate.)

Then go back and underline the settings that are most critical to your story. For each of these settings, answer the following questions:

- What purpose does this setting serve in the character's life?
- In your character's view, what is the dominant feature of this setting?
- What is your main character's emotional response to this setting? Does that change over the course of the story?
- How does this setting affect the action of the story?
- Is this setting altered in some substantial way over the course of the story?

Moving on

Key idea

Winding your setting details into the action – much as they appear in actual life – will help bring your story to life for your readers.

In Chapter 3 we explored the importance of action, and that holds true when describing your setting as well. Rather than having your character stand still in the doorway of a room and list its contents, have the character move through the room and interact with the objects to reveal them. Perhaps your awkward teenage boy will accidentally break a vase while waiting to meet his new girlfriend's father. Maybe a character desperate for cash will sneak a valuable item into her pocket. Maybe your allergy-prone character will plump up her grandmother's pillows and then have a sneezing fit from the dust.

All the while, focus on conveying details that contribute to readers' understanding of the story. If you are going to tell us that the room is dusty, then it should be dusty for a reason. Perhaps it's a signal that the grandmother is growing less able to care for things, and that the granddaughter may soon have to face a separation. Will the broken vase provide a handy excuse for the father to take an immediate dislike to the new boyfriend?

And, of course, keep in mind your viewpoint character, who acts as your filter. What would that viewpoint character notice in particular about the room, based on their interests and experience? Most younger children, for example, might recognize the furniture as old, but they would be unlikely to realize that the side table is a valuable antique. And a child who grew up in the city would be much more likely to cite an urban reference than a rural one when describing his surroundings in metaphorical language.

Study the key quote from Louise Erdrich's *The Birchbark House*. Erdrich evokes a distant time and place for readers, all through the experiences and actions of a young character with whom readers will still easily connect because of a shared desire to put play first and chores second.

Louise Erdrich, from *The Birchbark House*

'Moningwanaykaning, Island of the Golden-Breasted Woodpecker, sparkled innocently after that night of raw thunder and lightning. Omakayas woke and immediately began wondering. What had the storm done to the trees? What had the waves washed on to the beach? What interesting bits of wood that she could use for pretend dolls? What kind of day would it be? Were the little berries on the edge of the path ripe yet? An unpleasant piece of wondering came to her, too. Had her mother finished scraping and tanning that ugly moose hide or would she have to help her? Oh, she hoped not. How she hoped! There was a saying she hated. Grandma said it all too often. "Each animal," she would say, "has just enough brains to tan its own hide." Mama tanned the moose hide with the very brains of the moose and Omakayas hated the oozy

*feel of them on her hands, not to mention the boring, endless
scraping and rubbing that went into making a hide soft
enough for makazins.*

*'From a fire in the center of the bark house a thin curl of smoke
rose, then vanished through a crescent of sunlight in the roof. If
only she could escape with the smoke! She could already hear
Mama and Grandma outside at the cooking fires. They were
planning the day's work. In no time at all, that soaking moose
hide would be stretched on a branch frame and she would be
required to scrape at it with the sharpened deer's shoulder bone
that her mother kept in a bundle of useful things near the door.
Her arms would tire; they would feel like falling off. Her fingers
would go numb. Her back would hurt. The awful smell would
get into her skin. And meanwhile, all the little birds would find
the luscious patch of berries she alone knew about. By the time
she got that stupid old moose hide softened up, they would
have eaten every last berry. She must act. Quickly!*

*'The air was fresh, delicious, smelling of new leaves in the
woods, just-popped-out mushrooms, the pelts of young deer.
The air flowed in, rainwashed, under the strips of birchbark
walls she had helped sew together yesterday. Like a small,
striped snake, like a salamander, or a squirrel maybe, or a
raccoon, something quick, little, harmless, and desperate, she
slid, crept, wiggled underneath the sides of the summer house.'*

Get moody

You will also want to focus on creating a particular mood when
choosing descriptive details. If school is a character's safe haven
from an abusive home, then the language you use to describe the
school should reflect that. If, on the other hand, the character is
bullied at school, you will likely choose very different descriptors.

Don't just say it's raining: is it an icy, stinging rain or gentle spring
plops? Which one fits the mood you hope to establish for what's
happening in that portion of your story? Don't describe the setting
for a scary event with images of fluffy bunnies; all of your chosen
details should contribute to the mood you want to establish for
readers in regards to that setting, or that moment of action within

that setting. Think about choosing details as if you are selecting the background music for the movie of your story. Choose descriptive details that will play the right note for your readers.

Since the details you choose can help set a mood for that section of your story, they can also serve to cue readers that something in your story is changing. Study the key quote from *Jellicoe Road* to see how Melina Marchetta shifts the mood through her choice of contrasting details.

Melina Marchetta, from Jellicoe Road

'It's peaceful like this, on my back. A loving sun caresses my face and it wraps me in a blanket of fluffy clouds, like the feeling of my mother's hands when she first held me. For a moment I'm back there, in a place where I want to be.

'But then somewhere up-river, a speedboat or Jet Ski causes a ripple effect and miniature waves slap water onto my face, like an angry hand of reprimand, and the shock of it almost causes me to go under. I fight hard to stay afloat and suddenly I remember the feeling of fear in my mother's touch. Some say it's impossible because you remember nothing when you're five seconds old but I promise you this: I remember the tremble in my mother's body when the midwife first placed me in her arms. I remember the feeling of slipping between those fingers. It's like she never really managed to grab hold of me with a firmness that spoke of never letting go. It's like she never got it right.

'But that's my job.

'My body becomes a raft and there's this part of me that wants just literally to go with the flow. To close my eyes and let it take me. But I know sooner or later I will have to get out, that I need to feel the earth beneath my feet, between my toes – the splinters, the bindi-eyes, the burning sensation of hot dirt, the sting of cuts, the twigs, the bites, the heat, the discomfort, the everything. I need desperately to feel it all, so when something wonderful happens, the contrast will be so massive that I will bottle the impact and keep it for the rest of my life.'

Soundtrack

Look through your music collection. Some writers create actual playlists that evoke their story, a specific setting or a certain character, and play that music to help them write sections of their story. Choose songs and music that provide the appropriate musical mood or backdrop for different key settings in your story: this is your story soundtrack!

Less is more

Key idea

The 'less is more' rule often applies to adjectives. Sometimes writers are tempted to pile on adjectives to make sure readers see all aspects of a setting. But choosing one or two very telling adjectives will make those few descriptors stand out to readers, rather than getting buried in a long list.

We've already mentioned the importance of having your character interact with his or her setting, rather than just passively describing it. This approach evokes a strong sense of setting in readers while avoiding a particular risk: that a pages-long section of descriptive text will be labelled 'too boring' by young readers (who will then be tempted to give up on your book). This is another time when the less is more rule may apply: shorter descriptions can be more appealing.

Also consider what's happening at that moment of the story. During a moment of great crisis, for example, characters are highly unlikely to notice anything other than details connected directly with the crisis. Your character might feel the hot breath of his pursuer or the stickiness of his own sweat, but he's unlikely to notice the beautiful sunset.

All five senses

Writers often default to visual description, but there are numerous reasons to also include descriptions of smells, tastes, touch sensations and sounds when bringing your setting to life. Your readers, after all, live in and respond to a world that includes more than just the look of things. Creating that kind of world for your story will make them feel at home, even in the most exotic of fantasy lands, or encourage them to be fully present through all of their senses when engaged with reading your story. Reading can involve the whole body and mind!

Sensory experiences can also connect us to memories and emotions. For example, many people have experienced the close connection of smell and memory; one whiff of a particular odour from childhood can transport you back to a time and place you knew many decades ago. Food is often at the heart of family gatherings and special celebrations, as well as the source of battles between parents and children. And children often seem to experience tastes more intensely. Including taste descriptions in your story can evoke both an emotional and physical response. Including touch descriptors will more actively engage your young and very concrete readers in the reading experience.

SOUND OFF

Sounds can be very important in description, as books that have a strong oral quality make reading aloud a more engaging and satisfying experience. Picture books with sound effects are especially fun to read out loud. But even when reading to themselves, noises grab a reader's attention. Study the key quote from Julie Schumacher's *Black Box*, which demonstrates the power of sound descriptions for your setting; remove the noises (the screaming, the beep) from this excerpt, and this setting would feel quite one-dimensional.

 ## Julie Schumacher, from *Black Box*

'We can hear someone screaming as soon as we get off the elevator. At first it's hard to tell what the person is saying – the sound swells and fades, a high-pitched moving ribbon of noise – but as we walk down the narrow hallway (my mother reaches for my hand), I can hear the word "Out" and then "Out of here" and then "Let me out."

'We hang up our coats and lock my mother's purse and my father's keys in a metal locker. The screaming rises and falls. My mother glances at my father, and I can tell what she's thinking. We should have left Elena at home.

'We have to walk through a metal detector. The button on my jeans sets it off with a beep, and a security guard with a sagging belly gestures toward me and waves a wand up and down in front of my stomach. "Any knives?" he asks.

"What?' My brain is numb because of the screaming. "Letmeoutletmeoutletmego." It fills the hall and seems to suck up the air all around us.'

PICTURE BOOK PARTICULARS

 ## Focus point

A generally given piece of advice for picture book writers is to leave the visual details to the illustrator unless they are essential to the story.

It's sound advice for all writers to incorporate all five senses. But the non-visual senses offer special opportunities to picture book writers. After all, there will be an illustrator whose job it will be to portray the visual aspects of your story. But it is more difficult for an illustrator to portray the way something smells or sounds.

If your picture book character's purple room is her core conflict or is the one setting detail that best portrays her personality, then you will certainly describe it. But if your character's room colour has nothing to do with the story, then you can leave its portrayal safely in the hands of the illustrator. After all, you must keep your word count low; you can't afford a single extra word of text.

And remember that different animals favour different senses. If your picture book features a dog family, they will likely pay particular attention to smells, or your owl child will have exceptional hearing.

As already noted, picture books are read-alouds, and sound descriptions give readers a chance to incorporate sound effects to make the reading experience more entertaining. And young children are extremely sensory and concrete; they experience the world with their entire bodies. They may choose to reach out to stroke something when the story includes a tactile description or to pretend to sniff when a story relays a particular scent. Engaging all of their senses truly engages them in the experience of the book.

Study the key quote from Cynthia Rylant's picture book *The Relatives Came* to see an example of how Rylant incorporates smell, taste and even texture.

Cynthia Rylant, from *The Relatives Came*

'They had an old station wagon that smelled like a real car, and in it they put an ice chest full of soda pop.'

I'm sensing something

For this activity, choose a setting that has primary importance to your story. It might be a place where the character regularly experiences conflict, or her place of refuge, but it should be an instrumental location.

Since you will close your eyes as a key part of this activity, read through the instructions in their entirety first so you know all of the required steps. Review the instructions until they are clear. Then go ahead and follow the instructions.

- Open a computer file or have a pen and paper at hand.

- For now, you are going to focus exclusively on the sensory cues your imagination provides. When you understand the instructions, close your eyes and relax.

- Imagine that the inside of your head is the key setting you have chosen. Allow yourself to wander around this setting and experience it with all of your senses.

- Now, focus on what you see while inside the world of your story. Is it a colourful, enticing world? Is it a crowded, chaotic environment? Is it bleak and empty? Is it shadowy and frightening? Look around until you are fully immersed in the sights of your setting.

- Transition from seeing to hearing the world of your story. What sounds can you hear? Voices, music, animals, traffic, a burbling stream or a babbling baby? Perhaps if your setting takes place in an historical time, you will notice the absence of sounds that you are accustomed to in the contemporary world. Listen as intently as you can until you are submerged in the sounds of your setting.

- Move on to touching and experiencing the tactile sensations of your world. How does the air feel? What are the textures surrounding your character? Allow yourself to stroke an imaginary bedspread or feel the sharp edges of a rocky path under your bare feet. Thoroughly experience the touch sensations of your setting.

- Take a deep sniff. What does your setting smell like? Is there a faint odour from the pizza left to rot under the bed or the unwashed socks? Does the air in your fantasy land carry a faint hint of mint? Is there a particular smell that evokes a deep-seated memory for your character?

- Are there taste sensations within your setting? The coppery taste of blood as your character is smashed up against a locker in the school hallway? A snack that your character eats when they're feeling depressed? What tastes are a part of the world of your story?

- Open your eyes and as quickly as you can, write down all of the sensory details you can remember from the activity: sights, sounds, touches, smells and tastes. If you find you have a hard time capturing details the first time you try the activity, repeat it again.

If you find yourself struggling to imagine another key setting in your story, repeat the activity using that setting as well.

Get it right

Focus point

As a fiction writer, you have the leeway to embellish or change real-world details to better serve the story you are trying to tell. But for your story to ring emotionally true, you need to faithfully capture some essence of reality for your readers.

Research is a key part of creating a setting. It's especially critical for realistic fiction – but even science fiction, for example, is fed by an understanding of actual science. You will likely get away with building your fictional character a fictional home on a street that doesn't actually exist. But it's a much different thing to have your character growing a palm tree outdoors in a region that suffers from bitter winters. Your readers will most often accept the first scenario and reject the second in a work of realistic fiction. So, if you do alter a real setting, do so with discretion and intention.

Don't overlook the 'time' aspect of setting when considering authenticity. The current standards for historical fiction to accurately reflect a time period are especially high. While reviewers and educators (your book's gatekeepers) will accept an invented character as long as their existence is plausible in your historical setting, they are less tolerant of certain setting inaccuracies. Unless it's a work of historical fantasy, your character can't have convenient access to technology that wasn't yet invented, medical treatments that hadn't yet been tried, or hold attitudes that didn't yet prevail (or at least, not without some highly plausible explanation). As much as possible, the eighteenth century should look and feel like the true eighteenth century, and not like a costume drama.

You can consider yourself something of an authority when writing about a place you have lived for a substantial amount of time, and on contemporary life. Some writers choose to stick to settings such as these that they know well. But even when writing a story set in your home town, you may need to interview others to fill in the blanks in your own experience. Does part of your story take place in a school? If you haven't been in school since you were a young person yourself, you will want to talk with children or educators about the realities of school today. There are key differences from when you were in school, and relying on your own memories isn't enough.

Some writers choose to write about places and times that they haven't experienced first-hand. Ideally, you will actually be able to travel to the location of your story and immerse yourself in your surroundings. But given that airfare is expensive and time travel isn't widely available, you may not have that chance. In those cases, you can still make your setting come alive in an authoritative way via research. Work to find respected sources such as museums or scholarly documents, or people who have lived in the foreign setting you have chosen. See whether you can find first-hand accounts such as diaries or letters that provide personal insights (although not always accurate, these often contain a wonderful sense of local colour and anecdotes). Double-check details; often the things we believe to be true about foreign lands or ancient times are in fact apocryphal. Wherever possible, find at least three reliable sources to back up the facts you use to portray a place or time that aren't your own.

Start a photo book, a scrapbook or an image collage for your story. Search through magazines and online photo galleries, or create your own sketches for images that remind you of particulars in your setting. You might even cut out scraps of fabric to represent the curtains in your character's bedroom. For a story with an historical setting, you might visit a museum or find old photographs online. Go on an image hunt with your digital camera, looking for visual cues that might belong in your setting. Even if you're writing a fantasy, you might find objects at a toyshop to photograph, or search for particular colours that evoke the mood of your setting. Keep adding to your collection as you continue to write your story, and use it for inspiration whenever you're feeling stuck or need to submerge yourself in your setting.

Worldbuilding

Key idea

Whether it is a place they have visited many times or an invention of your own imagination, it is your job as a writer to make readers feel as if they have a grasp of what it is like to make a home in your intriguing world.

All writers must build a world for their characters, and their readers, to inhabit – and it may very well be a world readers have never before experienced. Perhaps it is a distant country or an ancient time. Perhaps a reader has always lived in the city, and your story has a rural setting. Perhaps it is just a world where there is no family structure or rules in place, and a reader comes from a strictly supervised home.

Worldbuilding has additional challenges when you're inventing a world that doesn't actually exist. When creating a story that will be labelled science fiction, fantasy, paranormal or dystopian, writers are building from scratch. They must bring their world to life while still serving the story they are trying to tell. And there is likely something about that world that will have a dramatic impact on the character and the conflict they are facing, so it must be carefully constructed.

When worldbuilding, you must focus on more than just sensory impressions. You must give readers the necessary clues to decode this strange new world you are asking them to visit. Some of the questions, such as how the magic works, are specific to certain genres such as fantasy. Other questions are important to any kind of fiction. What are the social structures and politics that make up this place? What role does technology play? Is the world in some way corrupt or at risk, and how does that affect your character and your story?

In Kristin Cashore's *Graceling*, the notion that certain people are 'Graced' plays a critical role in the story and in the life of her main character, Katsa, who is Graced herself. Study the key quote. It's a passage where Cashore helps readers understand more about the realities of life in the *Graceling* world – an understanding they will need to decode the story as a whole.

 ## Kristin Cashore, from *Graceling*

"'I give you fair warning," Oll said as they cleared the camp of their belongings. "This lord has a daughter Graced with mind reading."

"'Why should you warn us?" Katsa asked. "Isn't she at Thigpen's court?'

"'King Thigpen has sent her home to her father."

'Katsa yanked hard on the straps that attached her bag to her saddle.

"'Are you trying to pull the horse down, Katsa," Giddon said, "or just break your saddlebag?"

'Katsa scowled. "No one told me we'd be encountering a mind reader."

"'I'm telling you now, My Lady," Oll said, "and there's no reason for concern. She's a child. Most of what she comes up with is nonsense."

"'Well, what's wrong with her?"

"'What's wrong with her is that most of what she comes up with is nonsense. Or useless, irrelevant, and she blurts out everything she sees. She's out of control. She was making Thigpen nervous. So he sent her home, My Lady, and told her father to send her back when she became useful.'"

'In Estill, as in most of the kingdoms, Gracelings were given up to the king's use by law. The child whose eyes settled into two different colours weeks, months, or on the rarest occasions years after its birth was sent to the court of its king and raised in its king's nurseries. If its Grace turned out to be useful to the king, the child would remain in his service. If not, the child would be sent home. With the court's apologies, of course, because it was difficult for a family to find use for a Graceling. Especially one with a useless Grace, like climbing trees or holding one's breath for an impossibly long time or talking backward. The child might fare well in a farmer's family, working among the fields with no one to see or know. But if a king sent a Graceling home to the family of an innkeeper or a storekeeper in a town with more than one inn or store to choose from, business was bound to suffer. It made no difference what the child's Grace was. People avoided a place if they could, if they were likely to encounter a person with eyes that were two different colors.'

MORE WORLDBUILDING BASICS

Key idea

Avoid trying to build an entire world all at once. Your reader will be overwhelmed and likely confused. Let them experience the world a piece at a time as the character interacts with it.

You'll want to build your world slowly as your character interacts with it. Make sure that your reader has the key details they need to understand each section of story. But don't stop the action for endless pages of description.

You are the rule-maker of your invented world. But even a fantasy world has to follow some kind of logic. Once you establish a rule – perhaps that magic works only with the aid of a wand or another magical device – then you must stick to this rule. If you suddenly solve a character's problem halfway through the book by disclosing some convenient new magical ability, then you run the risk that readers will feel betrayed that you held out on them earlier in the story.

You will also want to hint at the type of story you are telling early on. If you are bending the laws of science, or if there is magic involved, provide a hint of magic within the first few pages. Readers like to feel they are in on the kind of story they have chosen, and might feel confused or frustrated if they think they are reading a realistic story and suddenly magic appears six chapters in.

And just as you are tracking details about each of your characters, don't forget to track the details you assign to your world as well, whether in a notebook or a computer file. Building a world is a big task, and there's a lot to keep track of!

Map it

Can you map out the world of your story? Do you know how the various kingdoms of your fantasy are geographically oriented? How far is it from your character's house to the cave in the woods where he goes to hide? Just how big is the school, and how many floors are there?

Choose an aspect of your world that still seems murky in your mind, and draw a map to help you illuminate it.

Ground your readers right from the start

Grounding your readers is about giving them sound footing right from the opening of your story. It brings your world to life for your readers when they first open your book, and gives them a sense of confidence that that world will be there when they next return to your story. Grounding your readers tells them they will be in capable hands if they choose to allow you to guide them through your world until the story's end.

You don't need to provide an enormous amount of setting detail in your story's opening, but readers should start to sense that the action is happening in a particular place and time. You might include a hint of something magical to signal a fantasy setting. You will likely include a few key details that tell readers your story takes place during a different time in history if that's the case. Action and conflict are still key in your story's opening, but you can ground them in your setting as well by providing a few key details mixed into that action.

Putting it all together

For the 'Hook your reader' snapshot activity in Chapter 3, you wrote three different possible opening paragraphs for your story. Now it's time to add the additional discoveries you've made about your character (in Chapter 4) and your story's landscape!

Review those three possible opening paragraphs. Choose the one that you now think is the most powerful – or create a new one, if you want to take a different approach. For this activity, you will expand that opening, paying particular attention to grounding your readers in the place and time of your story while still kicking off the action.

If you're writing a picture book, set a goal of 200 words for this activity and expand your story opening. If you're writing a longer piece, set a goal of 500–1,000 words and do likewise.

Workshop

1 Review

For the 'Putting it all together' snapshot activity, you expanded the opening to your story. Considering all that you have learned so far, rate your opening on the following (1 being the lowest score, 10 being the highest):

- I ground readers in my setting while still opening with action. ☐1 ☐2 ☐3 ☐4 ☐5 ☐6 ☐7 ☐8 ☐9 ☐10

- The descriptive details I chose establish a particular mood.　① ② ③ ④ ⑤ ⑥ ⑦ ⑧ ⑨ ⑩
- My descriptions evoke multiple senses.　① ② ③ ④ ⑤ ⑥ ⑦ ⑧ ⑨ ⑩
- My worldbuilding is effective.　① ② ③ ④ ⑤ ⑥ ⑦ ⑧ ⑨ ⑩

2 Close-up

I ground readers in my setting while still opening with action

- Does my story kick off with action (emotional or physical events that actively engage readers)?
- Do I include setting details that give my readers a sense of place?
- Do I include setting details that give readers a sense of time?
- Does my character move throughout the setting and interact with objects in it?
- Are the setting details interspersed with action?

Bearing in mind your response to the questions above, what could you change in your story opening to better ground your readers while still actively engaging them? Modify the opening accordingly.

The descriptive details I chose establish a particular mood

- Does my story opening establish a particular mood?
- Does that opening mood make sense given my overall story concept and the character's mindset when the story opens?
- Does that opening mood make sense given my target audience (for example, you might not choose to create a very spooky atmosphere if your audience is very young children)?
- Do the setting descriptions I use contribute to establishing that mood?

Bearing in mind your response to the questions above, what could you change in your story opening to better establish an appropriate mood? Modify the opening accordingly.

My descriptions evoke multiple senses

- How many sound descriptions have I included?
- How many smell descriptions have I included?
- How many taste descriptions have I included?
- How many touch descriptions have I included?
- How many sight descriptions have I included?

Bearing in mind your response to the questions above, do you need to make changes so that there is a greater variety or balance of senses represented? Modify the opening accordingly (note: you do not have to include all five senses, just a variety of senses).

My worldbuilding is effective

- Have I researched any setting details that are based on factual information?
- If the story is a genre such as fantasy, have I included a hint of this?
- Have I included any details my readers must have about my world to comprehend the story's opening action and conflict?
- Have I remembered not to overload my readers with too many details too quickly?

Bearing in mind your response to the questions above, is your worldbuilding effective? Modify the opening accordingly.

3 Re-review

Now read your revised work and re-rate the following from 1 to 10:

- I ground readers in my setting while still opening with action. [1] [2] [3] [4] [5] [6] [7] [8] [9] [10]

- The descriptive details I chose establish a particular mood. [1] [2] [3] [4] [5] [6] [7] [8] [9] [10]

- My descriptions evoke multiple senses. [1] [2] [3] [4] [5] [6] [7] [8] [9] [10]

- My worldbuilding is effective. [1] [2] [3] [4] [5] [6] [7] [8] [9] [10]

Where to next?

We have covered many of the elements that make up a successful story: theme, plot, conflict, character, dialogue, point of view and setting. For the next chapter, we're going to shift our attention to something else that is of primary importance to your story's success: how you can make steady writing progress.

6

Develop writing habits

We began this guide by focusing on some key aspects about the world of children's book writing and publishing. Then we examined several writing craft topics: theme, conflict, plot and structure, characters, point of view, dialogue, setting. We'll tackle additional matters along both of these lines in future chapters.

But, for this chapter, we're going to turn our attention to another topic that will have an equal impact on your goal to write a children's book: developing your writing process. Process has to do with the way you approach the writing act, the habits you work to ingrain so that you regularly get words on the page. It is about satisfying the most basic definition of being a writer: a writer is someone who writes, not just someone who dreams about writing.

Isn't inspiration enough?

 Renowned young adult writer
Markus Zusak

'I find writing extremely difficult. I usually have to drag myself to my desk, mainly because I doubt myself.'

Writing a children's book is an enormously fulfilling proposition. But if you have begun to sense that it also requires a lot of time and energy, your assessment is correct! So how do you keep yourself motivated to continue writing for the period of time that will be required? Based on the numerous guides that focus on defeating writer's block, it appears that an initial desire to write isn't enough. You must also learn how to keep producing creative work, even once your early ambition loses its shine or what once sounded easy starts to seem like it will require real effort. Or, as can happen with writers at all levels, you lose confidence in your abilities.

If you find yourself eager and excited to tackle your writing at every opportunity, that's fantastic. As my father often says, 'If it ain't broke, don't fix it.' If your current writing habits make you a productive, energized writer, then, by all means, continue them! Read through this chapter with an eye towards refining your habits in a way that will make you even more successful at meeting your writing goals. And with the thought that if you hit a snag – a time when you suddenly find writing a chore, something to be avoided or even scary – then you will have some tactics at hand to try.

But if you find yourself unsure how to actually get started, or for some reason are fighting to get words on the page, then I promise that you are not alone. In my years of working with and teaching writers professionally, I have seen many writers, at all levels, struggle with the act of writing. Some have received negative external feedback that has paralysed or discouraged them. Still others have found that the project in front of them is more difficult than they anticipated, and they're ready to give up. I have heard, over and over, many variations on the question: 'Why can't I just WRITE?'

The question is not limited to new writers or to unpublished writers: sometimes, it's just hard to follow through on a creative pursuit.

At such times, having strong writing habits in place, or even a few tricks to fall back on, can prove to be the difference between dreaming about writing, and actually being a writer.

Key idea

You can cultivate concrete practices now that will keep you writing even when you someday feel blocked, lack inspiration or have moved past the initial first flush of excitement.

Think like a writer

The first habit to instil in yourself is to think like a writer whatever else you're doing. Train yourself to notice things: details in the landscape, people's behavioural tics, how teenagers talk to each other when they don't know that anyone is listening. Pay particular attention to children who are your character and readers' ages. When you're in shops or watching the news, take special notice of trends that affect, or are affected by, children.

Carry a small notebook and pen with you to take quick notes when you note anything interesting. Train yourself to act as if you are reporting on the world around you, particularly the parts of it that especially concern children. Try a test trip to the mall or park. What do you notice when you're thinking like a writer?

Is it better to start small?

Some people assume that it's easier to write something short, such as a picture book or an easy reader. Or they think writing children's books in general will be easier, because they are for young readers. But the truth is, these projects have their own unique challenges. Some writers have no trouble filling many pages full of words, but then labour and sweat to cut those many words down to the spare text that a picture book requires. In other words, what is easy for one writer might prove very difficult for another.

It can also be difficult to make progress on a manuscript for which you have no passion. While you are still learning the basics of the writing craft and how to stay motivated, you will likely have more success if you choose a project that energizes and inspires you, whether short or long. Choose a project targeting a children's book category that you are genuinely enthusiastic about, because you may need to draw on that enthusiasm later when the act of writing seems tough.

A NOTE FOR THOSE WORKING WITH SHORT PROJECTS

If you are writing a project that requires few words, there's a chance you'll find yourself finished with your first draft before you've finished this chapter. A completed picture book may require dozens of revisions, so finishing that first draft certainly doesn't mean you'll be finished with your project at that point! But since we won't be tackling the revision process until a later chapter, you may choose to hold off until then to rewrite your first draft. If that's the case, then – when you have finished that initial first draft – take the opportunity to revisit some of the other ideas you considered in Chapter 2. As necessary, move on to writing a first draft for others of those ideas as you work through the activities found in this chapter. Many of the picture book writers I know juggle multiple projects at once, and this will give you multiple possibilities to choose from when we do reach the chapter that focuses on revising.

Give it a try

 Key idea

It can take a long time to develop new habits, and what feels awkward the first few attempts may prove to be eminently useful once you have become accustomed to the practice.

The intention of this chapter is to introduce you to a variety of possible writing practices and habits that you can adopt to help you be a productive writer. Not all of the activities will work equally well for everyone. But I encourage you to give each activity a try – ideally, try them more than once, as suggested.

Along with allowing you to sample different practices and identify some that might be helpful for you, another goal of this chapter is for you to begin making substantial progress on your children's book project. Many of the activities up to this point have focused on pre-writing exercises, the type of writing that helps you brainstorm and prepare to write. None of that has been wasted effort, I promise you. But at a certain point, you need to dig in and write, even without having all the answers or skills in place. Part of learning to write is simply learning *by* writing, mistakes and all. So view this chapter and the activities presented here as an opportunity to make clear progress on your children's story. If you have followed the guide up to this point, you have the basic craft tools in place to be able to do so. Now the key is for you to invest some time in drafting. It may take you awhile to work your way to the end of this chapter if you follow through on the suggested writing activities, but that's OK.

Looking ahead, you can also hold some of these practices in reserve. At a later time, when your circumstances have changed, your inspiration has seemed to desert you, or you are focusing on a different kind of writing project, you may find that what used to keep you writing no longer works. When that happens, revisit these suggestions to find a new approach that gets you back to making progress on producing pages.

Put writing first

Newbery Medal-winning author Kate DiCamillo

'I always quote Dorothy Parker: "I hate writing. I love having written." And so every morning, it's the first thing I do when I wake up. And every morning, I wake up and think, "Oh, God. I don't want to write today." But I just go ahead and do it anyway. And then for the rest of the day, I can think, "Oh, I got that done." And then I start the battle over again the next morning…'

Many writers laud the advantages of establishing a writing practice where you spend your first waking hours, most days of the week, writing. Sometimes it's a matter of trying to engage one's subconscious by capturing the remnants of your night-time dream state. But there can also be a more pragmatic reason. Other demands on our time and energy always pop up. By tackling your writing project first thing, you are ensuring that the later demands that so often come up during your day don't derail your good intentions to write later.

First thing

Set your alarm for a half-hour before you usually rise in the morning. As quickly as you can when the alarm goes off, pick up your pen or start your computer and begin drafting the next section of your children's story, beginning at whatever point you last left off. If needed, you can quickly read the last couple of paragraphs you had written before, to re-immerse yourself in the work, but don't stop to revise anything. Your focus should be on writing forward. Don't try to clear your head or organize your thinking first; just jump into writing. Stick with it even if it seems like all that's appearing on the page is nonsense. The key is to keep writing for the full 30 minutes.

Try to complete this activity on at least three different mornings. At the end of each session, note where you began and then finished writing for that day. Then take a few brief notes about that particular writing session. Did you find it difficult or exhilarating to get words on the page that day? How much writing did you get done? Was it hard to get started, but easier to write once you got going? Were there outside factors that affected your writing? Was it easier on the first or third day?

After three sessions, look over your summaries for each session. Are there any conclusions you can reach? Here are some questions to consider:

- Does 30 minutes a day feel like too much or too little time to set aside for a writing session?
- Were there any factors that made it easier to write one day over the others?

- On the days you wrote, did you have a feeling of accomplishment because you had honoured your writing goal that day?
- Would it be feasible for you to continue to write three to five mornings a week?
- What have you learned from this experience about your own writing process and goals?

Morning pages

Creative practice guru Julia Cameron, from *The Right to Write*

'The tool I ask you to undertake now is the most profound writer's tool I have devised or experienced. Called "Morning Pages," this tool is the bedrock of a writing life. Morning Pages bear witness to our lives. They increase our conscious contact with spiritual guidance. They prioritize our days while they miniaturize our censor, allowing us to write more freely and effectively. So what, exactly, are they?

'Morning Pages are three pages of daily longhand writing, strictly stream of consciousness. They are about anything and everything that crosses your mind. They may be petty, whiny, boring, angry. They may be cheerful, illuminating, insightful, and introspective. There is no wrong way to do them. You simply move your hand across the page while writing down whatever comes to mind.'

Several of my students have sworn by the value of Cameron's kind of morning writing practice – in effect, journaling in the morning rather than working to make progress on a specific writing project.

But, to be honest with you, if I were the one reading this guide instead of writing it, I would be writing off my chances of success as a writer at this point. As much as I trust and respect the fact that morning writing sessions – whether taking DiCamillo's or Cameron's approach – are a sound practice for many writers, the reality is that I am not a morning person. It's likely that, if getting up earlier than absolutely necessary was a prerequisite to being a writer, then I'd be selling shoes somewhere.

Because the practice does work for many writers, I hope you have already given – or will give – the idea of regular morning writing sessions a fair test. But if mornings simply won't work for you, then by all means try another time of day. The key will be to keep your commitment despite the other demands that gather as your day goes on.

As a night owl myself, I love to write very late at night, once things are quiet and there are few distractions. I get a second wind late in the evening, and I channel that energy into a writing session.

 Key idea

Are there certain times of day when you feel particularly creative? When do you have your best energy? Don't waste that time doing the laundry. If you apply your highest-energy, highest-creativity time to your writing several days a week, even if it's only a few minutes a day, you'll find you can make regular progress on your work.

Keep showing up

 Focus point

Persistence is one of the most critical traits for long-term success as a writer. Every level of writer faces frustration when writing seems harder than it should. Every writer faces rejection. Learning to persist despite those things is a requisite for the writing life.

There will likely be days when inspiration has grabbed hold and your words flow smoothly and almost effortlessly. And then there will be other days – the dark days – when writing feels like an onerous task, a seemingly impossible chore, and you will question why you ever wanted to do such an unrewarding thing. The writers who succeed over the long run are those who write in either case.

For long-term success, you want to depend on more than inspiration. You want to develop writing habits and practices that you can fall back on even when it's a bad writing day. Many writers say that the key for them is to write on a regular basis: for a set amount of time, for a set number of days every week – no matter whether they are inspired to write that day or not.

A page a day keeps writer's block away

Many writers, even those with very limited writing time, have finished entire novels by adopting a regular writing practice. As an example, writing one page a day – maybe around 250–300 words double-spaced – would mean that it would take a bit over 200 writing days to finish the first draft of a 60,000-word manuscript. Even accounting for days off, research days, unproductive days and false starts, that means that even a one-page-a-day writing habit makes it perfectly possible to complete a novel's first draft in a year.

Set aside a block of writing time, and write one new page (300 words) for your children's book. You can review the writing you have done before, but your goal is to generate one page of all-new writing, rather than a revision of already-existing writing, by the end of your session. Try this activity three different days at whatever time of day you choose.

How long does it take you to complete one new page? Could you commit to setting aside that amount of time two days a week? Five days a week?

Time or word count?

Creative coach Rosanne Bane, from *Around the Writer's Block*

'Because word counts cannot account for all the work we do throughout the entire creative process, overreliance on them can demoralize us and generate the very anxiety and resistance we need to avoid.

'This is why I tell my students and coaching clients to keep word counts if they wish while they're drafting, but they will be best served by evaluating their Product Time throughout all stages of the creative process not by how many words or pages they write or how good the writing is, but simply by whether or not they show up.'

When setting a daily or weekly writing goal, should you go by time spent, or by the number of words written? The truth is, there's no one right answer.

Long-time creative coach and writing process teacher Rosanne Bane is an advocate of setting a goal to write for a specific amount of time for a regular number of days each week. She is adamant that even individuals with highly demanding lives can successfully meet their writing goals this way, even those who are able to set aside only 15 minutes a day. In Bane's experiences, gained through working with a wide variety of writers, those who keep the commitment to show up for their writing on a regular basis find that in turn, their writing shows up for them.

Committing to a specific amount of writing time allows for the fact that not all stages of the creative process lead to lots of (or any) words on the page. If what you need to do to move forward on your project that day is to spend some time researching factual information, Bane asserts, then spending your allotted time on that is still 'writing' – even if you haven't increased your word count at all. Perhaps you are writing a picture book, where it can take 30 minutes just to find five absolutely perfect words. Or perhaps your time will be spent editing your picture book, and you'll actually end up with fewer words than you started with at the end of that day's writing time! In Bane's view, it is time spent more than word count that matters.

On the other hand, the US National Novel Writing Month (NaNoWriMo), which takes place every November, is based on the idea that striving to achieve a specific word count can be highly productive and motivating. The event inspires hundreds of thousands of writers around the world to attempt to write the first draft of a novel (50,000 words) in just a month. Through a combination of an intense (but reachable) deadline and a broad support network, many writers have found they are able to crank out a first draft for a novel in only a month. These novels may not represent great writing when 1 December rolls around but investing in this November outpouring of words works as an important starting point for many writers. For some of them, it serves to help them reach the stage where they have developed enough of their novel that they are then able to continue to refine it.

Writing 50,000 words is more than many writing hopefuls ever achieve, and is a testament to the fact that the combination of word count and deadline can be powerful. And while many of NaNoWriMo works are never published, the organization does cite many success stories, including several children's and YA titles.

National Novel Writing Month website

'Over 250 NaNoWriMo novels have been traditionally published. They include Sara Gruen's Water for Elephants, Erin Morgenstern's The Night Circus, Hugh Howey's Wool, Rainbow Rowell's Fangirl, Jason Hough's The Darwin Elevator, and Marissa Meyer's Cinder.'

Focus point

Writers who successfully achieve their writing goals take different approaches. You may need to experiment for a while to find which approach works best for you. But many successful writers share two common elements: they regularly set aside time for their writing and they find that setting a specific goal – whether word count, page count or time spent – for their writing output is helpful.

On retreat

When I need to draft and capture as much as possible of a story in rough form, particularly for a longer work, I crave long blocks of writing time. I want to be able to fully immerse myself in the world of my characters and their concerns, and that doesn't happen in just a few minutes. Once I am immersed, my writing seems to increase in speed, so that these longer sessions prove enormously productive. Could you stretch a 15- or 30-minute writing session to one or more hours instead, once or twice a week?

Writing retreats have also proven to be enormously helpful when I am completing a longer writing project or want to make substantial inroads on some work. I make good use of 15-minute blocks for certain stages of the writing process (brainstorming, researching, revising, editing). But a more extended period of concentrated time proves invaluable when I want to make significant or speedier progress on a piece.

Several hours strung together are great. But if it is ever possible for you to try a true writing retreat, that can be especially productive. Some writers are able to travel to an isolated spot, a place without the distractions of everyday life, and spend days or even weeks there. But my budget and responsibilities don't allow for that. Instead, I find ways to arrange a home retreat. I have to be a bit brutal in clearing out the people in my life, my other work responsibilities, and temptations such as reading a good book. But if I can do that for an entire weekend, I can make substantial progress.

Once you have arranged the time, clear away life's distractions. Don't check email or your social media accounts. Turn off your phone or ask the people in your life to honour your time by calling only if it's an emergency. Do the laundry and the dishes beforehand so family members don't nag at you. Stock up on easy-to-prepare meals. As much as possible, plan ahead so that your weekend retreat time can be devoted almost exclusively to writing.

The other key is to prep your writing for your writing time. Plan your retreat for a point when you have already done enough brainstorming and research so that your ideas are simmering and you have a foundation for your work.

As you are writing, take breaks when you get stuck or you grow tired, but continue to bring yourself back to the keyboard (or the notepad) and allow the world of your story to be your world for that period of time.

Stealing time

Sit down with your calendar and a notebook or an open computer file, and an open mind. Your goal is to find time you can steal from your regular schedule and reassign as writing time. This may require a trial-and-error approach and compromises. Many people feel that their life is too busy. They have other people who count on them and may need to be coaxed to change their expectations as well. But if you are serious about wanting to write, it is critical that you identify where there are blocks of time that you can set aside for writing.

First, look for smaller blocks of time. Can you continue to set your alarm for a half-hour earlier in the morning? Could you stay up for an extra 30 minutes after your family has gone to bed? If you sit outside the school gates, waiting to pick up your children every day, why not keep a notebook with you? Can you take 15 minutes out of your lunch hour at work to write? Could you give up that hour of TV or time on Facebook? Can you allow yourself to pick up takeout dinner a couple of nights a week? Could you leave the children with a babysitter for a couple of hours on a Saturday afternoon? Can you hand off a regular chore to somebody else to do, paid or unpaid, so you can redirect that time to writing?

Make a list of any of these ways or others that would allow you to steal writing time on a regular basis. Put a checkmark next to items that would gain you 15 to 30 minutes a day (four or five days a week) – these slots can help you establish a regular writing routine. Put a star next to items that would allow for longer blocks of time (such as an entire weekend afternoon).

Then look for longer blocks of future time that might allow for a longer writing retreat. It's usually not easy to carve these blocks out of a busy life, but the writing rewards can be enormous. Pencil in some possibilities on your calendar. Make a list of things you would need to arrange in advance to allow yourself a retreat. What can you do now to start the wheels rolling for this to become a real possibility?

The right tools and space

You'll also want to consider the space and equipment that will help you best pursue your writing goals. Do you have a designated writing spot in your home that helps you be productive, or do you need to create one that has fewer distractions? Do you need to consider an ergonomically correct chair and desk? Do you have space set aside to store books and research materials?

There are both writers and scientists who will argue for the benefit of writing by hand. And certainly for journaling, brainstorming activities and short projects, longhand can be an aid to creativity and a way to avoid keyboard fatigue – not to mention how easy it is to have a notebook and pen on hand at all times. In fact, if you typically write only on a computer, try writing by hand the next time you find yourself stuck, and note how it seems to tap into different parts of your awareness and creativity.

But, for practical purposes, if at all possible you will want your own laptop computer that is Wi-Fi ready. Accessing the Internet is key for research, networking with other writers and submitting your work. While some writers who take on long projects do write by hand, there are others who can't imagine tackling something of length without utilizing a keyboard. And however you draft your work, a computer will streamline your revision process.

If having to negotiate writing time for the shared family computer is a barrier to your writing, then purchasing your own laptop may be more than just a luxury. Another trick when you find yourself stuck or uninspired is to switch up your writing environment. It's handy to have your own laptop when you decide to search out a coffee shop, a park or a library as a change of pace.

 ## Make a commitment

Compare your experiences with the 'First thing' and 'A page a day keeps writer's block away' activities. Do you feel your writing time was more productive when you wrote with a time goal ('First thing') or with a word-count goal ('A page a day keeps writer's block away')?

- Make a commitment to work on your children's story in the coming week.

- Decide how many days you will write.
- Decide your writing goal for each session. Set a minimum of either 15 minutes, or one new page (300 words), per session. If your experiences so far have shown you that you are ready for a bigger challenge, you can commit to more. It is better to set a lower goal that you will achieve than an overly ambitious goal that you will fail at.
- Track your sessions to see if you have honoured your commitment or note the obstacles that stood in your way.
- After one week, schedule the next week. Plan around the obstacles you encountered. As you move forward with this guide, continue to set a weekly writing commitment each week. Work to find a routine that you can maintain and that allows you to make regular writing progress.

Things to avoid

Focus point

To be a successful writer, you can't wait to feel inspired.

Creative work is not always done well to a time clock or with efficiency in mind. The key is to build practices that help you make steady forward progress over time. Days that lead to 'bad' writing or that feel completely unproductive are a given; the key is to pick up and do it again the next writing day.

The writing habits that prove most effective for you may be different than those that work for someone else. But there are two common issues that I've seen derail many of my writing students – problems that with some advance warning you may be able to avoid.

First of all, don't expect too much of your initial efforts. Some writers become so tangled up in expectations of writing brilliant first drafts that they end up not writing at all. Even if you're not sure what to write, or exactly how to write, allow yourself to just get started. Write something that you can improve through revision. Write something that will need work, so that the process teaches you how to write a stronger first draft the next time. That's how you will move on to become a better writer.

Don't wait to be inspired. It's a lot of fun to write when you feel energized to do so. But the creative muse is fickle and doesn't always show up on demand. Stick to your writing commitments, inspiration or not. And when you have kept your commitments despite not feeling at all motivated to do so, give yourself a small reward as recognition of that fact.

Key idea

First drafts are often very rough. The purpose is to get something on paper that you can refine. Revising, or working to improve your first draft, is the bigger part of any writer's job – but you can't revise without first drafting.

Enlist your brain

There are times when life keeps you from writing at all. In those times, I have found that I can enlist my brain to work on my writing even when I'm not able to actively engage with it.

Here's how it works. Identify a specific question you have about your story. It might be something like, 'What is motivating Character A to act in this way?' Or, 'What unusual tactic could Character B try to solve her problem this time?'

Then, assign the question to your brain. I'm very explicit about doing this; I actually say something goofy like, 'Brain, here's my question…' After that, you don't need to consciously revisit the question. But in my experience, sometime within the next few days or weeks, an answer will come floating up.

This isn't a substitute for writing – but it is a way to keep your fingers on the pulse of a project when life has made other demands. You can also ask these questions while you are keeping your regular writing commitments, but need some help finding an answer.

Try it out: identify a question you have about your story, and assign it to your brain to see what happens!

Workshop

1 Review

For this chapter, you tried different approaches to generating new portions of your children's story. In this workshop, you are going to focus on some of that writing. If you are writing a picture book, work with your entire draft (if you have more than one manuscript-in-progress, choose just one). If you are writing a longer work, choose a section of five to eight pages. Considering all that you have learned so far in this guide, rate that section on the following (1 being the lowest score, 10 being the highest):

- I am breathing life into my characters. [1] [2] [3] [4] [5] [6] [7] [8] [9] [10]
- My story is compelling. [1] [2] [3] [4] [5] [6] [7] [8] [9] [10]
- I am grounding readers in an intriguing place and time. [1] [2] [3] [4] [5] [6] [7] [8] [9] [10]
- My selected point of view is effective. [1] [2] [3] [4] [5] [6] [7] [8] [9] [10]

2 Close-up

I am breathing life into my characters

- Am I making it clear that my main character wants or needs to gain or change something?
- Are my characters taking action in ways that reveal their personalities?
- Am I including dialogue that reveals something about each character's individuality?
- Do my characters feel authentic and are they more than just stereotypes?

Bearing in mind your response to the questions above, what could you change in this story selection to better breathe life into your characters? Modify the selection accordingly.

My story is compelling

- Is the core conflict of the story obvious?
- Is this conflict relatable for my target readers?

- Is there action – emotional and/or physical – on every page?
- Is the plot simple enough for the reading abilities of my targeted readers (if I have chosen a category)?
- Have I avoided bogging down the action with too much back story or description?

Bearing in mind your response to the questions above, what could you change in this story selection to make your story more compelling? Modify the selection accordingly.

I am grounding readers in an intriguing place and time

- Am I continuing to bring my story setting to life?
- Do I give readers clues about the specific time and place of my story?
- Do I use a variety of senses in my descriptions?
- Am I building a world that the reader will want to regularly visit?

Bearing in mind your response to the questions above, what could you change in this story selection to better develop your setting? Modify the selection accordingly.

My selected point of view is effective

- Have I chosen a viewpoint character that my target readers will find compelling?
- Am I writing consistently in either first person or third person limited?
- Am I remembering to consider my viewpoint character as the filter for my story?
- Am I avoiding head-hopping?
- Is my point of view choice effectively conveying the story in the way I want it told?

Bearing in mind your response to the questions above, do you need to alter your overall point of view choice? Even if you aren't going to alter your choice, what do you need to change to use point of view more consistently and effectively? Modify the selection accordingly.

3 Re-review

Now read your revised work and re-rate the following from 1 to 10:

- I am breathing life into my characters. ⬚1⬚2⬚3⬚4⬚5⬚6⬚7⬚8⬚9⬚10

- My story is compelling. ⬚1⬚2⬚3⬚4⬚5⬚6⬚7⬚8⬚9⬚10

- I am grounding readers in an intriguing place and time. ⬚1⬚2⬚3⬚4⬚5⬚6⬚7⬚8⬚9⬚10

- My selected point of view is effective. ⬚1⬚2⬚3⬚4⬚5⬚6⬚7⬚8⬚9⬚10

Where to next?

Now you have had a chance to start building your writing muscles through regular writing workouts. While you continue to practise those good habits, we're going to shift our attention back to the craft side of writing – this time, to choosing the most powerful language for your story, conveying it in a way that will most deeply engage your readers.

7

Find the right words

You've learned about many of the overarching craft issues that will help you shape your story: developing your characters, structuring a plot, building a world that draws in your readers. In this chapter, you will narrow your focus to words themselves: how to choose them to best tell the story you are driven to tell. You will learn tactics that will help you shape your language in ways that will make your writing more vivid, compelling and relatable for your target audience.

Stay on track!

In the last chapter, I encouraged you to set and meet weekly
writing goals. Continue to do this to build your regular writing
habits. If you need to do so, you can count the writing activities in
this chapter as part of meeting those writing goals. If you haven't
already done so, review (or set) your writing goals for this week.

Show, don't tell

One of the most commonly shared pieces of writing advice is to
'show, don't tell'. But trying to figure out what exactly that means,
and how to do it, can be confusing. The good news is, you have
already started to shape your writing in a way that shows instead of
simply tells.

Showing is revealing to readers who your characters are and what
they are experiencing through what they do and say, not just by
summarizing how they look or feel. Showing is creating active
scenes, using specific and compelling details, crafting dialogue that
rings true, and carefully establishing a mood.

If showing creates such a strong reading experience, does that
mean that telling is always wrong? Not at all. Telling takes fewer
words and is sometimes necessary to move the story along. There
are times, for example, when you simply need to make a transition
from one place or time to another, when it is fine to summarize
what is happening. If you need to move your character down the
hallway to the kitchen, and the hallway is of no importance, then
there's no reason to bring the hallway to life. You can simply tell
readers that the character walked down the hallway. But if it is
during this transition from one room to another that the character
makes a major realization, then you will want to show rather than
tell readers about that moment, to bring them inside the experience
of the character, hallway and all. As the writer, you have the power
to be selective in choosing which moments are those that need to be
shown, and which can simply be told.

Put readers to work

Telling your readers 'Nick felt sad' doesn't engage readers or encourage them to empathize with him. In fact, be wary of the word 'felt' – or its other verb forms such as 'feels' or 'was feeling' – as these often signal a moment of telling instead of showing.

But showing readers a scene where Nick hunches his shoulders, wipes his eyes, runs to hide in his room, and then chokes back sobs, will allow them to infer that Nick is sad without you ever using the actual word. They will become more deeply engaged, both in the process of reading, and in Nick's emotional state, through your use of the showing style of writing.

In Laurie Halse Anderson's *Speak*, the main character Melinda has suffered something so traumatic that she can't talk about it. But, as the story goes on, readers begin to put together the pieces of what has happened through Anderson showing them insights into Melinda's emotional state. Study the key quote to see how the author pulls it off.

Laurie Halse Anderson, from *Speak*

'I scurry out to the three-way mirror. With an extra-large sweatshirt over the top, you can hardly tell that they are Effert's jeans. Still no Mom. I adjust the mirror so I can see reflections of reflections, miles and miles of me and my new jeans. I hook my hair behind my ears. I should have washed it. My face is dirty. I lean into the mirror. Eyes after eyes after eyes stare back at me. Am I in there somewhere? A thousand eyes blink. No make-up. Dark circles. I pull the side flaps of the mirror in closer, folding myself into the looking glass and blocking out the rest of the store.

'My face becomes a Picasso sketch, my body slicing into dissecting cubes. I saw a movie once where a woman was burned over eighty percent of her body and they had to wash all the dead skin off. They wrapped her in bandages, kept her drugged, and waited for skin grafts. They actually sewed her into a new skin.

'I push my ragged mouth against the mirror. A thousand bleeding, crusted lips push back. What does it feel like to walk in a new skin? Was she completely sensitive like a baby, or numb, without nerve endings, just walking in a skin bag? I exhale and my mouth disappears in a fog. I feel like my skin has been burned off. I stumble from thornbush to thornbush – my mother and father who hate each other, Rachel who hates me, a school that gags on me like I'm a hairball. And Heather.

'I just need to hang on long enough for my new skin to graft. Mr. Freeman thinks I need to find my feelings. How can I not find them? They are chewing me alive like an infestation of thoughts, shame, mistakes. I squeeze my eyes shut. Jeans that fit, that's a good start. I have to stay away from the closet, go to all my classes. I will make myself normal. Forget the rest of it.'

Showing instead of telling

For this activity, you are going to practise showing three different words – the words in boldface below (in three separate pieces of writing, not combining the words in the same piece). You can create a straightforward description of the word, or develop a scene where the word is featured in some way; your approach is not the issue. The goal is to convey the essence of that word to readers so that they feel like they are experiencing it.

Here's the catch: you can't use any form of the word in boldface, or any form of the list of words underneath the word in question. This will force you to think outside the box and bring the word to life in a way other than using the most obvious language.

Here is your first word:

Thunderstorm

- Rain
- Thunder
- Lightning
- Shower
- Wet

So, you are to bring the word 'thunderstorm' to life for your readers without using any of these words, or forms of these words such as 'storm', 'raining' or 'showering'.

Once you have finished the first word, move on to these two words:

Covet

- Want
- Desire
- Yearn
- Possess
- Have

Haunted

- Ghost
- Spirit
- Spooky
- Obsessed
- Supernatural

Action words

Key idea

With the exception of dialogue tags, where 'said' is sufficient, you will want to make sure that you have chosen the strongest and most telling verbs, those that perfectly capture the action of that moment in the story.

Action has been a recurrent theme in this guide. And what better way to make sure that your story is action-packed than to focus in on the action words – your verb choices. Work to include a wide variety of interesting verbs rather than defaulting to the same old choices. Avoid the passive sentence form when possible: rather than saying 'The book was read by Sarah,' say, 'Sarah read the book.'

When you are tempted to use an adverb, ask yourself whether you could instead find a stronger verb. For example, instead of saying, 'He moved quickly,' try 'scampered' or 'dashed' or 'barrelled'. Each of those verbs is much more descriptive and establishes a unique visual picture for the reader in a way that 'moved quickly' doesn't. In fact, if you find you tend to overuse adverbs, train yourself to notice every time you write a word ending in '-ly' as so many adverbs do. Each time you write '-ly', challenge yourself to instead find a more powerful verb.

Word power

There are other ways to power-pack your word choices beyond using active and varied verbs. In Chapter 5, we discussed the importance of choosing setting details that establish a mood. This is true when you are describing characters and action as well. Have you been selective in your use of adjectives, selecting one or two of the most telling descriptors instead of burying the most intriguing in a long list? Do your word choices support the dominant impression you want to create? Is your language 'heavy' when the character is dealing with grief, for example? Is it light-hearted during a moment of playfulness?

Work to make your language fresh and original, just as you worked to make your story concept feel fresh and original. Your readers may quickly become bored if you fall back on well-worn clichés. Think about making word choices that challenge readers to see something in your story as if for the first time.

Also make sure that your language reflects the timeframe of your story. You don't need to convert to authentic Shakespearean English if you're writing a story set in the Renaissance, but it shouldn't sound like eavesdropping at the local mall, either. Using a modern turn of phrase in a novel set in historical times will quickly make readers question your authority. Using outdated slang in a contemporary story will also give your readers pause. Make sure each of your word choices contributes to making your story world as believable as possible.

Weighing your words

Choose a point in your story when your character makes an important realization. It might be when he comes to recognize the obstacle that stands in the way of getting what he wants. It might be when she realizes something that shows her the true magnitude of her problem. It might be a surprise discovery about another character. Whatever it is, choose a section full of heightened action and emotions.

With what you now know about showing instead of telling, and choosing strong verbs and other power-packed words, write that scene in a way that puts readers inside the experience of that story moment as fully as possible.

Move it along

Your word choices, along with your sentence structure, can also affect the pace of your story. At a point of heightened action and tension, you will want to consider choosing shorter words and shorter sentences. This staccato style of writing will read more quickly, which mimics the speeded-up, even breathless sense you want to create at such a moment in your story. On the other hand, when you reach a point where you want to slow your readers down and invite them to contemplate what is happening, then you can choose longer words and lengthen your sentences.

Other languages

At times, you may want to add some authenticity by having characters use a few words or phrases in a language other than English. You will want to keep these relatively short; longer passages will frustrate and confuse young readers. The important thing is to provide some context so that young readers can interpret the meaning of the words you do use. Perhaps one character could greet the other by saying 'Hello' in the alternate language; when the second character answers 'Hello' in English, readers will infer what the original greeting means. Or perhaps a character could use a term that means 'grandfather' or a term of endearment that is obvious because of the relationship of the two characters.

Remember your target audience

 ## Key idea

Words are the building blocks of your writing. Remember your target audience when you consider which building blocks to use.

The children's book category you are writing for will also have an impact on your language choices. If, for example, you build your easy reader story using words that are strong and vivid – but also of a difficult vocabulary level – then your story won't succeed with your target audience. You will want to write in a way that is clear and direct enough for readers in your target category to follow. You might want to glance back over Chapter 1 to remind yourself of the target audience and key considerations for each children's book category before you read through the category-based considerations below.

Picture book writers can get away with using more difficult words because an adult will be reading the book to a child. However, the read-aloud experience will be disrupted if the child listener has to stop the adult to ask 'What does that mean?' too often, so use difficult language judiciously. Ask yourself, is this truly the best word, or would a simpler one work just as effectively? Is there something the illustrator could include in the artwork to cue the young listener as to what the unfamiliar word means? Is it a word that sounds wonderful when read out loud, and therefore enhances the picture book experience? The read-aloud quality of the word is perhaps your primary consideration when choosing the language for your picture book.

Easy readers have the most stringent demands in regards to word choices. Often, your word choices will be dictated by concerns other than what is the most evocative word; for example, you may be working to reinforce a particular vowel sound, and make your word choice based on that instead. Or you may choose to repeat a word to reinforce it, rather than searching for an interesting synonym (as you would likely do when writing for older readers). Review the 'Resources when writing for new readers' section in Chapter 1 to remind yourself of some of the tools available to you when writing for this level.

Chapter books can use somewhat more challenging language than easy readers, but you will still want to remember that your readers are fairly new to the task and choose words accordingly.

Middle grade novels provide an opportunity for you to make more demanding language choices. However, you will still want to choose words that are 'child-friendly' in regards to being relevant to the interests of young readers. For example, few young people are intrigued by the world of adult finance, so you would be unlikely to use a metaphor based on that world. Young readers are much more likely to respond to a metaphor based on their own interests and passions. The other concern that arises for this age level is the use of swearing or inappropriate language. While the readers in this age category, especially those at the upper end, will likely have had some exposure to 'colourful' language, it is rarely tolerated by the gatekeepers of middle grade novels. Susan Patron's *The Higher Power of Lucky* received wide media coverage not only because the title won the coveted Newbery Medal in 2007, but because the author chose to use the word 'scrotum' in an anatomically accurate manner. In the judgement of some adults, the use of the word, however accurate, was offensive.

Young adult books may very well feature swearing and harsh language that will disconcert some parents and other gatekeepers. But authors argue that to authentically represent a teen voice and the gritty situations YA characters find themselves in, these language choices are necessary – and that a cleaned-up version would be condescending or ring false to the teenage audience. Since readers at this level are often choosing and purchasing their own reading material, the ultimate test is what these readers believe makes the story most compelling. Writers have made a variety of choices in regard to this issue, sometimes avoiding rougher language and sometimes fully embracing it; if you are targeting this category, you will want to consider where you fall as a writer and make your decision accordingly.

Focus point

Challenging young readers with interesting new words will enhance your story. The key is to try to achieve a balance. Remember your target readers and choose the words that will best stretch those readers' imaginations while bringing your story fully to life – while still allowing those readers to succeed in their reading experience.

To rhyme or not to rhyme

Some writers assume that rhyming verse is the ideal approach, or even a requirement, when writing for young children. And, when done well, rhyming verse is wonderfully playful and memorable, especially for read-aloud texts. This has led many a writer to emulate authors such as the ever-popular Dr. Seuss and try their own hand at the rhyme game.

However, many editors say that they refuse to consider rhyming verse. Why the disjoint between what appears to be so popular and what editors say they want? Because editors also report that they are inundated with manuscripts composed in dreadfully executed rhyme. Well-done rhyming verse appears effortless, so many people assume it is simple to write. And they overwhelm those same editors with manuscripts that reflect little craft or care, causing the editors to issue blanket anti-rhyme statements.

Sometimes it proves best to let go of the rhyming verse and tell your story without it. You may find that your story becomes much stronger without the rhyme. Other times, attempting to tell the story without rhyme convinces the writer that rhyme is necessary. I wrote one of my own picture books in rhyme, so I know how much fun it can be when it works. But I have also had the experience of trying to force a story into rhyming verse when it wasn't meant to fit. It wasn't until I finally tried it without the rhyme (six fruitless months later) that the story quickly came together.

If you are committed to trying your hand at rhyming verse, by all means do so. Just know that your standards must be especially high because of the editorial bias.

Key idea

Artfully done rhyming verse requires consummate storytelling skills *and* a finely honed poetic voice. In other words, rather than being simple to write, rhyming verse adds extra demands to your job as a writer. It requires a wonderful narrative and adds the additional requirement of rhyming verse strong enough to turn anti-rhyme editors into fans.

Rhyme-free

If your story is written in rhyming verse, you should always take the time to test whether the rhyme actually enhances it. In other words, you should now try writing your story in regular prose, without the rhyme. You may find that trying to write effective rhyming verse has been hindering rather than helping you write the story you are meant to tell.

METER MATTERS

This section and the next will be of special interest to those who do choose to write rhyming verse.

Effective rhyming verse is not just a matter of rhyming the last word of each line. You also need to consider meter. This means the arrangement of stressed and unstressed syllables in your lines. The number and pattern of stressed syllables typically stays consistent from stanza to stanza. It is OK to vary your meter at times, but it should be an intentional choice on your part, not something that happens by accident. Readers will hear the difference when the meter changes, so you might use the change to send them a signal to pay extra attention at that point in the story. You might also include a repeated change in meter as part of a larger pattern of the whole work, to keep the piece from becoming sing-songy.

If you are still learning to hear meter and trying to figure out how to scan your work to see whether you are writing it effectively, nursery rhymes can be a useful learning tool. You can also look online at the many helpful websites and blog posts that tackle meter, or study a poetry how-to book such as poet Mary Oliver's *Rules for the Dance*.

SOME RHYMING 'RULES' AND TIPS

- **Your story must still make sense** and be complete and compelling based on all of the advice covered in earlier sections of this guide. The need to make your rhyme work doesn't exempt you from telling a great story.

- **Don't force your rhyme.** Each individual sentence should make sense written as it is. Look for places you have inverted, or convoluted, your sentence to force the rhyme or meter (for example, 'No more writing should you do.') If it doesn't sound the way you would normally say it out loud in conversation, your verse will be ineffective.

- **Don't rely on near rhymes,** which are words that come close but don't actually rhyme, such as 'made' and 'rate'.

- **Make interesting, original choices;** relying on obvious or predictable rhymes will sound the editorial warning bell. However, archaic language is not the answer to original. Don't use old-fashioned language that will ring untrue to readers simply to satisfy your rhyme.

- **Don't rely on filler words or phrases** that are only there to make the meter or rhyme work. Just as with other picture books, you cannot afford unnecessary words. Everything must help move the story forward.

- I've stressed the need to read your work out loud many times in this guide. When writing in rhyming verse, it's also invaluable to **ask someone else to read the work out loud** to you – preferably someone who has never read it before. Listen for any place that they stumble or that the meter sounds different than what you expected.

Cultivating your voice

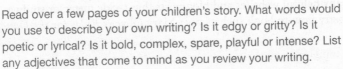

What kind of writer are you?

Read over a few pages of your children's story. What words would you use to describe your own writing? Is it edgy or gritty? Is it poetic or lyrical? Is it bold, complex, spare, playful or intense? List any adjectives that come to mind as you review your writing.

If you are struggling to come up with descriptors of your story style, think about what people have said in the past about other things you have written – even casual emails or letters. A friend might have given you a hint of how your writing comes across by saying something along the lines of 'I laugh every time I read one of your emails' (humorous). A teacher might have said, 'It's as if your words sing' (melodic or harmonious). Perhaps your writing has a spooky quality, as in 'Your stories send shivers down my spine.' Or maybe your work is quirky, as in 'You always catch me by surprise with your unusual outlook.'

Try to come up with at least three words that you believe describe your writing.

Key idea

Your voice is the unique way that you put together words to tell stories. It is a reflection of your personality, background, outlook on life and the way you use language. Your voice is a distillation of your essence as a person, reflected back to your readers through your writing.

When editors are asked to name the key elements they look for in a submission, more often than not 'voice' is towards the top of their list. We have already covered the need to develop your characters' individual voices. But these editors are referring to your overall voice as a writer. The list of words you came up with for the 'What kind of writer are you?' activity are likely a start at describing your writer's voice.

Think of your voice as your personal filter through which you refine your story. The more you write, the more developed that voice will become. And as editors' responses indicate, a highly developed voice can be extremely compelling. It is one of the key ways that a writer takes a core story that has been told many times before and makes that story her own. It is one of the reasons that readers return to a writer they love.

Some writers' voices are so intense and identifiable that they come to represent a certain style of writing. Or their readers will say that they can recognize the writer's voice even if the work is published anonymously. Study the key quotes featuring children's book writer Patricia MacLachlan and young adult author Francesca Lia Block. They each have strong – but very different – voices.

Patricia MacLachlan, from *Sarah, Plain and Tall*

'I wiped my hands on my apron and went to the window. Outside, the prairie reached out and touched the places where the sky came down. Though winter was nearly over, there were patches of snow and ice everywhere. I looked at the long dirt road that crawled across the plains, remembering the morning that Mama had died, cruel and sunny. They had come for her in a wagon and taken her away to be buried. And then the cousins and aunts and uncles had come and tried to fill up the house. But they couldn't.'

Francesca Lia Block, from *Weetzie Bat*

'Weetzie took the paper away. "Honey, I have something to tell you," she said.

'Weetzie was pregnant. She felt like a Christmas package. Like a cat full of kittens. Like an Easter basket of pastel chocolate-malt eggs and solid-milk-chocolate bunnies, and yellow daffodils and dollhouse-sized jellybean eggs.

'But my Secret Agent Lover Man stared at her in shock and anger. "You did what?"

'"The world's a mess," My Secret Agent Lover Man said. "And there is no way I feel okay about bringing a kid into it. And for you to go and sleep with Dirk and Duck without even telling me is the worst thing you have ever done."

'Weetzie could not even cry and make Kleenex roses. She remembered the day her father, Charlie, had driven away in the smashed yellow T-bird, leaving her mother Brandi-Lynn clutching her flowered robe with one hand and an empty glass in the other, and leaving Weetzie holding her arms crossed over her chest that was taking its time to develop into anything. But My Secret Agent Lover Man was not going to send Weetzie postcards of the Empire State Building, or come visit every so often to buy her turkey platters at the Tick Tock Tea Room like Charlie did. Weetzie knew by his eyes that he was going away forever. His eyes that had always been like lakes full of fishes, or waves of love, or bathtub steam and candle smoke, or at least like glasses of gin when he was sad, were now like two heavy green marbles, like the eyes of the mechanical fortune-teller on the Santa Monica pier. She hardly recognized him because she knew he didn't recognize her, not at all.'

Some writers are known for having a quirky or unusual voice. If that is the kind of voice that you naturally fall into, then cultivate it. But the goal is not to force yourself to sound anything other than yourself. Work to cultivate the natural elements of your voice, whatever they are: for the right reader, 'serene' or 'poetic' can be just as powerful as 'cutting edge' or 'hip'. If you find yourself forcing a particular voice, you may be pushing too hard. The goal is to allow your natural voice to emerge through practice, rather than forcing out your voice in a heavy-handed way.

New writers can also get the impression that there are good and less good voices. For example, someone who is naturally funny might assume that real writers are more serious in tone. However, since your voice is a reflection of who you are as a person, you also want to sound authentic and use your natural gifts. Perhaps your sense of humour is a tool that will allow you to tackle a serious topic in a way that makes it accessible to young readers who would otherwise be wary of a book that is too heavy or dark. Just as you are multifaceted and full of nuances as a person, your voice will be multifaceted and full of nuances too; even funny people have to grapple with life's dark realities. What can you share with young readers that will show them that there are a variety of ways for differing people to take on trouble?

Mimic the masters

Identifying and developing the qualities that go into a writer's voice is a complex process. Emulating the voices of other writers can be a great way to learn some of the intricacies that go into voice. Devote time to studying and even mimicking the voices of the writers you greatly admire – and then work to develop your own voice by allowing your own personality to emerge as you write. Your voice will ring false if you've based it solely on someone else.

For this activity, you are going to try on the voice of celebrated children's book writer Roald Dahl. Study the key quote from Dahl's book *Matilda*. Then choose one of the characters from your own children's story. You are going to write a description of that character, mimicking as best you can Roald Dahl's voice while you do so.

Keep in mind that you're not copying Dahl; you're mimicking his voice. You do not necessarily need to choose an antagonist in your story. You won't use the same words or images that Dahl does. Instead, you'll study the kinds of words and images that he uses, how he structures his sentences, and the mood he establishes, and then try to create a passage with a similar feeling for your own character.

Roald Dahl, from *Matilda*

'Miss Trunchbull, the Headmistress, was something else altogether. She was a gigantic holy terror, a fierce tyrannical monster who frightened the life out of the pupils and teachers alike. There was an aura of menace about her even at a distance, and when she came up close you could almost feel the dangerous heat radiating from her as from a red-hot rod of metal. When she marched – Miss Trunchbull never walked, she always marched like a storm-trooper with long strides and arms aswinging – when she marched along a corridor you could actually hear her snorting as she went, and if a group of children happened to be in her path, she ploughed right on through them like a tank, with small people bouncing off her to left and right. Thank goodness we don't meet many people like her in this world, although they do exist and all of us are likely to come across at least one of them in a lifetime. If you ever do, you should behave as you would if you met an enraged rhinoceros out in the bush – climb up the nearest tree and stay there until it has gone away.'

Focus point

There are two key ways to cultivate your writing voice. First, read a wide variety of other writers, paying particular attention to those whose voices reach off the page to grab you by the throat, head, or heart. Second, write, write and then write some more. Nothing else will develop your voice like exercising your writing muscles.

Getting a taste of different voices

For this activity, you're going to try another approach to testing out different writing voices, with the ultimate goal of learning more about your own natural voice.

The terms below are from the world of wine tasting, as defined by the Wine Folly blog (winefolly.com/tutorial/40-wine-descriptions). You are going to create a writing voice to fit each of these terms.

'BUTTERY

A wine with buttery characteristics has been aged in oak and generally is rich and flat (less Acidity). A buttery wine often has a cream-like texture that hits the middle of your tongue almost like oil (or butter) and has a smooth finish....

FLAMBOYANT

A flamboyant wine is trying to get your attention with an abundance of fruit....

STEELY

A steely wine has higher acid and more sharp edges. It is the man-ballerina of wine....'

Madeline Puckette, Wine Folly blog

Write a page in the first voice (buttery), and then in the second (flamboyant) and then in the third (steely). You can write about anything you choose – your family life, your favourite season, your dream home, your biggest disappointment, your last vacation. Since these terms are from the word of wine tasting and not necessarily used to describe writing, you should feel free to be playful and creative – there is no right way to do this activity. The goal is to think about writer's voice from a completely fresh perspective, so that through this process of trial and error and elimination, you can come closer to understanding what is and is not your own true voice.

Once you have tried a page in each voice, reflect on the overall experience and answer the following questions:

- What voice was easiest for me to use?
- What elements of that voice are like my natural writer's voice?

- What voice was most difficult for me to use?
- What does that tell me about what is not my natural writer's voice?

You might also want to visit the Wine Folly website yourself, to see if there are other terms that more closely match your own voice, or to try your hand at testing out further voices.

Workshop

1 Review

For the 'Weighing your words' snapshot activity, you worked to write in a showing way while also including strong verbs and power-packed words. Considering all that you have learned so far, rate that scene on the following (1 being the lowest score, 10 being the highest):

- I did a good job of showing instead of just telling. [1] [2] [3] [4] [5] [6] [7] [8] [9] [10]

- I used varied and powerful verbs. [1] [2] [3] [4] [5] [6] [7] [8] [9] [10]

- I made intriguing and appropriate word choices. [1] [2] [3] [4] [5] [6] [7] [8] [9] [10]

- I am allowing my true writing voice to emerge. [1] [2] [3] [4] [5] [6] [7] [8] [9] [10]

2 Close-up

I did a good job of showing instead of just telling

- Are my characters revealing who they are through their actions and dialogue?
- Have I created active scenes where things happen?
- Have I used specific and telling details that engage readers' senses?
- Have I built empathy in my readers by putting them inside my characters' emotions?

- Am I allowing my readers to draw their own conclusions from the clues I provide rather than summarizing everything for them?

Bearing in mind your response to the questions above, what could you change in this scene to show instead of tell? Modify the scene accordingly.

I used varied and powerful verbs

- Have I written in active rather than passive form?
- Are my verb choices powerful and active?
- Have I avoided repeating the same verb too often (unless it was for the specific purpose of learning through repetition in an easy reader)?
- Have I appropriately broken the rule above by sticking to 'said' for dialogue tags?

Bearing in mind your response to the questions above, what verb and sentence structure changes could you make in this scene? Modify the scene accordingly.

I made intriguing and appropriate word choices

- Do my word choices help establish the mood I want for this section of my story?
- Does my language feel fresh and original instead of predictable and clichéd?
- Are my setting descriptions appropriate to the timeframe of my story?
- Am I structuring my sentences to match the appropriate pacing for this portion of the story?
- Are my word choices appropriate for my target audience and chosen category?

Bearing in mind your response to the questions above, what words could you change in this scene? Modify the scene accordingly.

I am allowing my true writing voice to emerge

- Is there a sense of personality to the voice?
- Does the voice ring true as my natural voice?

- Does the voice avoid feeling forced, over the top or heavy-handed?
- Is the voice consistent throughout the selection?

Bearing in mind your response to the questions above, what could you change in this scene? Modify the scene accordingly.

3 Re-review

Now read your revised work and re-rate the following from 1 to 10:

- I did a good job of showing instead of just telling.

  ⬜1 ⬜2 ⬜3 ⬜4 ⬜5 ⬜6 ⬜7 ⬜8 ⬜9 ⬜10

- I used varied and powerful verbs.

  ⬜1 ⬜2 ⬜3 ⬜4 ⬜5 ⬜6 ⬜7 ⬜8 ⬜9 ⬜10

- I made intriguing and appropriate word choices.

  ⬜1 ⬜2 ⬜3 ⬜4 ⬜5 ⬜6 ⬜7 ⬜8 ⬜9 ⬜10

- I am allowing my true writing voice to emerge.

  ⬜1 ⬜2 ⬜3 ⬜4 ⬜5 ⬜6 ⬜7 ⬜8 ⬜9 ⬜10

Where to next?

You have put a lot into creating a first draft for your story. In this chapter, you paid particular attention to choosing the words that will best bring that story to life. Next, we'll continue with that kind of careful scrutiny, this time applying it to revising your first draft so that it becomes an even more compelling read.

8

Revise your work

Congratulations! If you have done your best to carry out the activities presented so far in this guide, you have a lot to celebrate. My experience is that many, many people believe that they *could* write a children's book – but that few of them actually carry through on that notion in the substantial way that you have.

So what's next? It's the thing that perhaps more than any other part of the writing process separates the writing dreamers from the writing doers: revision. And while it may be tough to hear that you're not as close to being finished as you perhaps thought, there is some good news. For many writers, revising isn't an onerous task. It's actually their favourite part of writing! The revision process allows you to fully explore all the dimensions of your idea and often leads you to completely unexpected – but deeply satisfying – places with your work.

Re-vision

The art of revision is just what it sounds like: to discover a new vision for a piece of writing. It is the act of imagining your work anew, refining it in a way that allows it to be as fully realized as possible. Revising your work will mean 'big picture' changes to your overall story, and more focused changes such as substituting a stronger word for one that isn't working hard enough.

You have already practised revising your work: many of the workshop activities that have concluded each chapter of this guide required you to revise. This chapter will simply provide a more systematic overview of the revision process.

Is it the right time for you to revise?

Some readers of this guide, especially those working on shorter pieces, will have finished one or more first drafts at this point. If you fall into this category, then select one of those completed first drafts as the manuscript you will focus on for the activities in this chapter.

Other readers of this guide, particularly those tackling longer works, will likely only be partway into their first draft. I encourage you not to judge yourself based on the speed of your writing. If you are writing on a regular basis, and doing your best to implement the advice offered here, then you are making steady (even if not speedy) progress.

But if you haven't yet finished your first draft, there may be some activities in this chapter that you can't yet carry out – because they require you to evaluate the entire completed arc of your story. You have a couple of options if you have not yet finished your first draft. You may decide that you want to complete it before you do further revising. If that is the case, then I recommend that you continue to read through this chapter now – but don't yet work through the 'Write', 'Snapshot' and 'Workshop' activities. When you have finished your first draft, MAKE SURE that you come back to tackle those activities. You can also go ahead and work through Chapters 9 and 10 while you are continuing to finish your first draft.

Or you may choose to go ahead and try as many of this chapter's activities as you can complete now, so as not to lose important momentum with this guide.

A word of warning

Bestselling author Anne Lamott, from *Bird by Bird*

'Almost all good writing begins with terrible first efforts. You need to start somewhere. Start by getting something – anything – down on paper. A friend of mine says that the first draft is the down draft – you just get it down. The second draft is the up draft – you fix it up. You try to say what you have to say more accurately.'

I'm something of a perfectionist. That trait makes writing the first draft difficult for me, because drafting is about just getting words down, whether they are the right words or not. Revising, on the other hand, is a chance to play with words and ideas and make them 'better' so it comes much easier to me.

When I'm working on a long project, I reward myself by taking some time to tweak earlier sections of the work before I settle into drafting new sections. Because of that, I can warn you about one danger that you will want to avoid: becoming so deeply immersed in revising an unfinished work that you never actually complete it through to the end.

Focus point

If you begin revising before you finish your first draft, be sure to focus some of your writing energy on completing your manuscript through to the end instead of just on revising – otherwise you may never finish that first draft.

Absence makes the head see clearer

 ## Children's writing teacher Laura Backes

'The most useful thing you can do, upon completing your manuscript, is to set it aside for at least a week and start on something else.'

Often the best first step in the revision process seems counter-intuitive: ignore it. Taking a break from your project before reworking it – sometimes just a few days is enough, and other times much longer is necessary – allows you the time and distance to gain critical objectivity on your writing.

This is not meant to be an excuse to abandon a project or to give up on your regular writing practice. While you're taking a break from the first project, go on to experiment with others.

 ## Take a break

Back up your computer files and print out a copy of your manuscript. Then set it aside for at least one week. Don't read it or focus on it during that time.

Then choose a completely different children's book category. It can be one that has intrigued you from the beginning of this guide, or it may be one that represents a personal challenge for you. Spend your regular writing sessions during that week trying to get a start on this alternate project. Remember that the earlier chapters of this guide may prove helpful.

Be playful and experiment! You may not choose to stick with this different form once the week is over, but you will learn a lot by challenging yourself to consider another target audience and category. Many children's book writers end up shifting from one category to another over the course of their career. Perhaps you will surprise yourself with what you discover during this week.

Think positive!

Revising requires applying a more critical, discerning eye to what you have written. Sometimes, particularly for people who are perfectionists, looking at a manuscript with a too critical eye can shut down your forward momentum completely; you can become so discouraged that you give up.

But revision should be a positive process: its goal is not to discourage or frustrate you. Remember that all writers need to revise if they want to grow their work and their skills. The fact that you are capable of recognizing potential areas of improvement is a sign of how much you are learning. Celebrate the progress you have already made by getting words on paper, and allow yourself to become enthusiastic about this opportunity to explore the work's potential. If you are willing to invest time in the revision process, you can make your story stronger. And you will become a better writer in the process!

Time and again, when I've critiqued someone else's manuscript, I'll point something out to the writer that seems vague or confusing to me, and he will shake his head sheepishly and admit, 'I knew that wasn't working. I just hoped maybe you wouldn't notice!' Trust your instincts. If you're guessing that something isn't working, you're probably right. Take the opportunity to refine the piece in a way that allows its potential to be better realized.

Another very common occurrence is that I will ask the writer I am critiquing a question about her manuscript, and she will start to explain what she meant to say. Remember that you will not be there peeking over the readers' shoulders to answer their questions! They will have only your printed words to rely on. There are times you will deliberately hold back information from the reader as part of building suspense, but that isn't what I'm addressing here. I'm talking about the kind of information that should be on the page for that section of your story, but that is instead stuck in your head. During the revision process you are identifying what things your readers must know to make sense of that section of your story – and whether you have neglected to make some of those things clear. Revision is your chance to empty the complete story on to paper so that readers can own it for themselves.

Key idea

Perhaps it is helpful to see revision as an opportunity to ask yourself two key questions: How can I bring this piece closer to its potential? And, what do I know about the story that isn't yet present for readers?

Read-through

Read through your work from start to finish (as much as you have completed so far). Try to think like a reader instead of as the writer of the piece. Dive into the work as if you have no idea what it's about or how the story ends. Avoid stopping to fix things; the goal is to gain an overall sense of how the story as a whole is hanging together.

When you're done reading, jot a few notes to yourself about your overarching impressions, questions and concerns. What worked well for you as a reader? What was vague or confusing?

The onion approach

Key idea

Breaking revision down into more manageable segments makes it much easier.

Once I have read through the entire piece and gathered an overall impression of it, I like to use the onion approach to revision: I think in layers to keep the process manageable.

Part of thinking in layers might mean tackling different revision tasks as separate steps. I might focus exclusively on developing a particular character throughout the entire story – and then, as a different step, focus exclusively on making all of the dialogue sound more realistic. Another sort of layering might be deciding that for one day's work I am going to focus exclusively on one scene.

Vocalize

I have lauded the benefits of reading your work out loud many times in this guide. Sit down with a printed copy of your picture book manuscript or the opening scene of a longer work. Read the work out loud. Jot a note every time you find a place that sounds awkward, is difficult to read out loud, doesn't sound like authentic dialogue, etc.

Organization is key

Key idea

Staying organized is a huge revision time-saver.

Even if the first draft is in longhand, I use the computer for my revision work – it allows for greater efficiency and organization. Within the computer folder for my children's book project, I create a folder called 'drafts'. And then each time I set out to begin a new revision, I do a 'save as' for my manuscript file and add the next higher number to the file name. For example, if my shortcut name for my manuscript is 'Fish', then I call my first draft 'Fish 1'. When I begin revising, I 'save as' and call the new version 'Fish 2', and so on. Sometimes, a later version doesn't work out, and this approach allows you to easily return to an earlier version.

I also keep scrupulous notes. While I am focusing on that day's revision goal, ideas or considerations always arise that affect different elements or sections. I keep a computer file labelled 'Revision Notes' open to capture all of these ideas. I don't want to forget about them. But if I allow myself to jump to another section or element every time I think of something other than what I'm focusing on, it makes me much less efficient. So as much as possible, after making a brief note, I try to remain focused on my original revision goal for that day's work. Then I return to my notes another revision day.

Finally, there are times when you will need to delete a portion of your manuscript that you really like – but that doesn't actually fit the story you are trying to tell. It can be hard to let go of these treasured bits, but a discerning writer learns to identify when something doesn't belong. It can help to know that you have safely stowed this bit of writing in case you need it at some later time. I keep a computer file called 'Great Bits' and transfer these deleted portions into that file for safekeeping.

Where do I start?

When tackling the revision process in layers, where should you begin? I recommend you start by addressing big picture concerns. They include considerations such as the following:

- Was your original idea big enough to carry the entire story?
- Does the story fit into one of the children's book categories?
- Would a young reader feel compelled by the story to stay up after the official 'lights out' time to find out what happens next?
- What is the reader left with when the story closes? Would they want to read it again?
- Is your character transformed in some way over the course of resolving the conflict?
- Does the story or the resolution feel clichéd?
- Does the resolution at the end of the story answer the questions raised for readers at the beginning?

Begin by considering 'big picture' concerns because they could require you to rework, delete or add large sections of writing. Once you have tackled the big picture issues, you might switch over to revising on a chapter-by-chapter or scene-by-scene basis, putting more focus on revising individual language choices. But there are times when a fresh start will make more sense than trying to go through and 'fix' everything that isn't yet working. In other words, you might choose to rewrite your story opening from scratch, rather than just tweaking it here and there. Some writers set aside their entire first draft and begin anew with the whole story; the first draft was a way for them to see the overall arc of the story, and they feel they will get better results with this fresh-start approach for their second draft.

Choose your category

Some writers set out from the beginning to create a story to fit a particular children's book category. Others may not be sure which category they want to target, and instead opt to make that decision after learning more about the story through writing the first draft. Whichever is true for you with this particular story, the revision process is your chance to evaluate your manuscript to see what category it best fits into – and to make the necessary changes to make sure that you are consistently signalling the same target audience.

Also consider the word count list below. These word counts are only general ranges; you will find exceptions with different publishers and certain types of stories. Graphic novels and novels in verse will have much shorter word counts; fantasies often have much higher word counts. You can also go to Renaissance Learning at arbookfind.com / http://www.arbookfind.co.uk/ to look up published books similar to your own and compare what their word count totals are.

Because recommended word counts do vary, I offer them here only so that you can determine if your manuscript is considerably outside the typical range. If it is, you may need to revise accordingly.

- Picture books: ideally under 550 words, definitely no more than 1,000 words
- Easy readers: 200–2,500 words
- Chapter books: 4,000–15,000 words
- Middle grade: 25,000–60,000 words
- Young adult: 45,000–75,000 words

Word count alone is not the way to determine which category your manuscript fits into. For example, your story might only be

800 words long. But if your main character is 11 years old and is worrying over the pressure of too much schoolwork, it's not likely to be a picture book or easy reader. Instead, it might be a magazine short story for eight through eleven-year-olds.

Focus point

Meeting publishers' expectations for a particular children's book category is more important when you are just starting out. Publishers are less likely to be open to something outside the norm from a first-time writer.

If you haven't already done so, now is the time to determine which children's book category your draft best fits into. Refer to the Chapter 1 guidelines, as necessary. If you are writing a picture book, do the 'Make a dummy book' exercise. If you are writing any other type of children's book, follow the instructions in 'Make a chapter summary'. If you are writing an easy reader that isn't broken into chapters, then substitute 'scenes' instead of 'chapters' as necessary in 'Make a chapter summary'.

Taking shape: Make a dummy book (picture book writers)

Because of reasons having to do with the printing process, most picture books are 32 pages long. This also includes opening pages such as the title page and the copyright page. So, although it can vary, the story in a picture book fits on to approximately 27 pages. English-language books almost always begin the story on a right-hand page, so for a typical picture book there might be this single right-hand page followed by 13 two-page spreads.

You are going to make a 'dummy' book that will allow you to mimic this layout as a revision tool.

*   Take seven pieces of printer paper, fold them in half vertically, and staple the folded edge to create a 'book'.
*   Print out the text for your picture book. Draw a line at the end of each action or major change in your story (for example, a

character enters or leaves, the setting shifts, the character realizes something new). Cut the manuscript at each line so that you have a hunk of text representing each action or change. Distribute the hunks of text throughout your dummy book, one for the opening right-hand page and one for each of the following 13 spreads (leave the back page blank).

- Jot down ideas of what the illustrations might look like for each spread; the text of your picture book should inspire potential illustrations for every new turn of the page. Does your text provide enough visual potential but still leave room for an illustrator to bring her own creative inspiration to the process? Could readers follow the story even without the illustrations?

- Now consider how the text fits on to the pages of your dummy book. Is there enough action or change to fill the whole book? Does one action require 200 words, and another take only ten words? Could you imagine an illustration that might go with each spread, and is it substantially different from the illustration on the previous spread?

- Do you find that each spread offers something that moves the story forward and compels readers to keep turning the pages? If not, what might you need to change, add or delete?

Make a chapter summary (other-than-picture book writers)

- List each of the following on a chapter-by-chapter (or, for short easy readers, scene-by-scene) basis for your story.
- How many pages long is the chapter?
- What is the day, date if applicable and time of day covered?
- Write a brief paragraph description of this chapter. It should include the major events that take place, the characters that appear, the locations and what new information the reader learns about the characters or the conflict.
- Describe an illustration that might accompany this chapter. Books for older readers may or may not be illustrated, but

the goal is for you to identify whether you have included enough cues for readers to form pictures in their own heads.

- Once you are finished, evaluate your summary. Are there chapters where nothing much seems to happen – that could potentially be deleted? Is one chapter three times longer than average, and perhaps needs to be broken into two? Does the summary reveal any problems with the sequence of your timing? Are there chapters without any reveals of new information? Are there chapters where readers will struggle to form pictures in their heads?
- Do you find that each chapter offers something that moves the story forward and compels readers to keep turning the pages? If not, what might you need to change, add or delete?

Keeping pace

Pacing is the speed at which your story moves. In Chapter 7, we discussed how short or long sentences can alter the pacing. Throughout this guide we have also focused on the need to include lots of action in your story. However, a story that is all action can overwhelm readers. You will want to periodically slow down your pacing to give readers a chance to reflect on and take in the importance of the action that has just taken place.

You can affect your pacing in ways other than sentence length. Including lots of details or description, flashbacks and characters' contemplations slows the pacing. Lots of action, and short scenes and chapters, speed up the pacing.

 ## Action map

You want the overall movement of your story to feel as if readers are climbing a hill towards the story's climactic moment – the point where everything teeters between despair and triumph for your character. Each time the character attempts to solve her problems and then fails, the intensity grows and the stakes are raised as readers 'climb the hill' along with the main character.

New problems arise, the conflict seems more insurmountable, and the climb grows tougher. Using pacing, you will periodically stop the story on a plateau – slow down the action – to give readers a chance to catch their breath and take stock during this uphill journey. Finally, readers will reach the peak of the story, after which the suspense drains out and the story slopes downhill to a satisfying ending.

Draw a map or illustration of the action in your story. Does your story follow this 'climbing the hill' pattern?

Leave them dangling

Young people often read a book in chapter increments; a parent might say, 'One chapter before lights out', or a teacher will read a book a chapter at a time in the classroom. Ending a chapter with a cliffhanger – where you leave the outcome dangling – pushes readers forward through your story. Chapter-ending cliffhangers create an exciting reading experience.

Especially for younger readers, it is also helpful if you briefly ground readers at the opening of each new chapter as a reminder of where the story left off at the last reading. This might be as simple as something like 'Fortunately the ghost didn't haunt Justin's dreams', reminding readers of the ghost's appearance in the previous chapter.

The kindest cut

Key idea

Deleting is one of the most critical revision tasks.

Deleting can happen on many different levels of your manuscript; some deletions will affect the entire big picture, and others will focus on cutting individual words that contribute to an overall sense of 'wordiness'.

In Chapter 2, you wrote a 'Dear Reader' letter in which you identified the most important takeaway that you want to impart to your young audience – your story's theme or big idea. This letter helped you identify the idea that would act as the focus for your entire story. Everything in your story should point back to that core focus in some way. Are there parts of your story that don't? They may be among the first items you'll need to cut.

Deleting could also require excising unnecessary characters. Could you easily condense two best friends or two different teachers into one, or are two truly needed? Do adult characters play too prominent a role, and could you downscale their importance or eliminate them entirely?

Deleting can mean cutting entire scenes or chapters that don't move the story forward. If they have too little action or don't add some new understanding for readers, they may not be necessary.

You may need to cut out large hunks of back story that make your story opening drag. Some of this might be worked into a later section of your manuscript, but only when the reader needs the information to appreciate the current action of the story. Identify the first key action in your story – could you delete everything that comes before that, and begin your story in that active moment?

Deleting will also include tightening your story by eliminating unnecessary words. Tightening is important in all stories – as we draft, we aren't always stopping to consider every word we commit to paper, and some of them will prove extraneous. But tightening is especially critical in picture books. When revising a picture book, you will challenge every single word of your text to make sure it belongs in the story or can't be left to the illustrator to portray.

Sometimes deleting is a straightforward task: removing something you recognize is not your best writing. But, other times, you must let go of work that is beautifully crafted, but that doesn't fit into your overall story. It can be tough for writers to let go of these characters, scenes and lines. But part of the revision process is learning to read your own work with objective – even pitiless – eyes. If any word, element or section does not truly fit into and strengthen the story you are trying to tell, then you must be willing to let go of it. Put it into your 'Great Bits' file for a possible later story.

What if, once again

In Chapter 2, we discussed the value of asking yourself 'What if?' in regards to generating possible ideas. The question is just as important, if not more so, when it comes to revision time.

Revising is a chance to be playful and turn your work on its head to ensure that you have not settled for a less surprise-filled and evocative story than you are capable of writing.

For this activity, make a list of 20 assumptions you have made about your story. They can cover a wide variety of story elements and concepts. Here are some examples:

- I assume that the story must be told in first-person point of view.
- I assume that Character A must be the viewpoint character.
- I assume that Character B must be a villain.
- I assume that the solution to the character's problem must be X.
- I assume that the setting must be Y.

In other words, all of the things that you once may have had to think through but perhaps now take for granted about your story could end up on this assumptions list.

Then go down the list item by item, and change each listing to a 'What if' question. In other words:

- What if instead of first person point of view, I told the story in third person limited?
- What if instead of Character A as the viewpoint character, it is Character B?
- What if Character B is not really a villain after all?

- What if, instead of the solution being X, it is Z?
- What if the setting changed to Q?

Review your list of 20 'What if?' questions. You might quickly dismiss several of the items. But there will likely be one or two that make you stop and think about new and exciting possibilities for your story. You might even want to test some of them out. For instance, why not try a section of your story using third person limited instead of first person, just to see how that works?

Before you settle, take some time to push yourself to be as creative and open-minded on your story's behalf as possible.

And then again

You can consider the earlier chapters of this guide as a kind of extended revision checklist. Refer back to each chapter as part of your revision process. In other words, when you are considering whether the characters in your first draft emerge as clearly as you hoped they would, review Chapter 4 as part of your evaluation process.

You have learned several different approaches to viewing your manuscript more objectively in this chapter. Based on those, you have likely identified a lot of necessary revision work. If your first draft is complete, move on to devoting your regularly scheduled writing sessions to tackling these revisions, with the goal of making the same steady progress with revising as you did when you were drafting.

Keep in mind that revision is rarely a one-time process. In fact, writers may rework their stories dozens of times before they are fully polished.

 ## Mary Kole, former literary agent and now freelance editor

'How much revision is normal? A whole lotta revision is perfectly normal, in fact, it is encouraged. Many authors routinely rewrite their entire books from scratch.'

Workshop

1 Review

This chapter provided many ways for you to evaluate your manuscript and identify its strengths and weaknesses; all of them provided vital information you will want to consider when revising. But for this workshop, you are going to focus on ten particular issues – the ten issues that over my many years of critiquing student work have proven to be the primary big picture problem areas evident in first drafts. If you can eliminate all ten of these problems, you will be well on your way to polishing your manuscript.

Considering all that you have learned so far, rate your first draft (or as much as you have finished) on the following (1 being the lowest score, 10 being the highest):

- I put readers inside the emotions and action of the story.
  [1] [2] [3] [4] [5] [6] [7] [8] [9] [10]

- The story will appeal to children or teenagers (not just adults).
  [1] [2] [3] [4] [5] [6] [7] [8] [9] [10]

- The story fits one of the children's book categories.
  [1] [2] [3] [4] [5] [6] [7] [8] [9] [10]

- The story starts off quickly.
  [1] [2] [3] [4] [5] [6] [7] [8] [9] [10]

- The tension of the story increases as it moves forward.
  [1] [2] [3] [4] [5] [6] [7] [8] [9] [10]

- The story has a clear focus.
  [1] [2] [3] [4] [5] [6] [7] [8] [9] [10]

- The story feels fresh and original.
  [1] [2] [3] [4] [5] [6] [7] [8] [9] [10]

- Point of view is consistent and effective.
  [1] [2] [3] [4] [5] [6] [7] [8] [9] [10]

- There is enough showing rather than just telling.
  [1] [2] [3] [4] [5] [6] [7] [8] [9] [10]

- If it is a picture book, the language is extremely concise and evokes illustration potential.

① ② ③ ④ ⑤ ⑥ ⑦ ⑧ ⑨ ⑩

2 Close-up

I put readers inside the emotions and action of the story

- Do readers feel a strong connection to my main character?
- Do readers feel as if they are participating in the story as it unfolds?

Bearing in mind your response to these questions, what could you change in your story? Modify the story accordingly.

The story will appeal to children or teenagers (not just adults)

- Does my main character share children's/teenager's concerns?
- Does my main character solve his/her problem without an adult taking over?
- Does my story avoid feeling overly nostalgic?
- Have I avoided writing a piece whose only goal is to teach children a lesson?

Bearing in mind your response to the questions above, what could you change in your story? Modify the story accordingly.

The story fits one of the children's book categories

- Are my character's age, the reading level, and the way the topic of the story is addressed all consistent with a particular children's book category?
- Am I on target with my word count?

Bearing in mind your response to the questions above, what could you change in your story? Modify the story accordingly.

The story starts off quickly

- Does the story start out with action?
- Is the conflict introduced within the first few pages of a longer book, or the first few sentences of a shorter book?

Bearing in mind your response to the questions above, what could you change in your story? Modify the story accordingly.

The tension of the story increases as it moves forward

- Does my character's conflict grow worse before it gets better?
- Do I maintain suspense until the final resolution?

Bearing in mind your response to the questions above, what could you change in your story? Modify the story accordingly.

The story has a clear focus

- Is there an underlying big idea driving the story?
- Does everything in the story point back to this focus?

Bearing in mind your response to the questions above, what could you change in your story? Modify the story accordingly.

The story feels fresh and original

- Is there some kind of surprise in the way the story unfolds or is resolved?
- Does the story feel different from other stories I've read on a similar topic?

Bearing in mind your response to the questions above, what could you change in your story? Modify the story accordingly.

Point of view is consistent and effective

- Does the point of view choice enhance the reading experience?
- Have I avoided head-hopping?

Bearing in mind your response to the questions above, what could you change in your story? Modify the story accordingly.

There is enough showing rather than just telling

- Do critical scenes come to life in a vivid way?
- Does the reader experience the story through the five senses?

Bearing in mind your response to the questions above, what could you change in your story? Modify the story accordingly.

If it is a picture book, the language is extremely concise and evokes illustration potential

- Is every single word necessary to my picture book?
- Will an illustrator find it easy to create a book full of varied and intriguing illustrations?

Bearing in mind your response to the questions above, what could you change in your story? Modify the story accordingly.

3 Re-review

Now read your revised work and re-rate the following from 1 to 10:

- I put readers inside the emotions and action of the story.
  [1] [2] [3] [4] [5] [6] [7] [8] [9] [10]
- The story will appeal to children or teenagers (not just adults).
  [1] [2] [3] [4] [5] [6] [7] [8] [9] [10]
- The story fits one of the children's book categories.
  [1] [2] [3] [4] [5] [6] [7] [8] [9] [10]
- The story starts off quickly.
  [1] [2] [3] [4] [5] [6] [7] [8] [9] [10]
- The tension of the story increases as it moves forward.
  [1] [2] [3] [4] [5] [6] [7] [8] [9] [10]
- The story has a clear focus.
  [1] [2] [3] [4] [5] [6] [7] [8] [9] [10]
- The story feels fresh and original.
  [1] [2] [3] [4] [5] [6] [7] [8] [9] [10]
- Point of view is consistent and effective.
  [1] [2] [3] [4] [5] [6] [7] [8] [9] [10]
- There is enough showing rather than just telling.
  [1] [2] [3] [4] [5] [6] [7] [8] [9] [10]
- If it is a picture book, the language is extremely concise and evokes illustration potential.
  [1] [2] [3] [4] [5] [6] [7] [8] [9] [10]

166

Where to next?

This chapter covered some of the tactics you can use to make your story more powerful, polished and complete. But as you tackle your potentially lengthy revision, you can also begin to engage in the bigger world of children's books. It is there you will find the support you need as you work beyond the pages of this guide.

9

Join the community

As someone who is writing a children's book, you are part of a large, worldwide children's book community. There are authors, illustrators, librarians, educators, university departments, organizations, publishers, booksellers, journals, bloggers and many other interested individuals and organizations who invest themselves in the creation, study or advocacy of children's books.

You can easily become an active participant in this children's book community even as an unpublished writer. Your exposure to others in this world will help you refine your work and your skills. You may also be looking ahead to submitting your work for publication. Becoming an active part of the community is a smart move as you consider this step – networking will help you make valuable connections that may someday prove to be enormously helpful in your publisher search.

Keep up your writing sessions!

As we discussed in the last chapter, writing and revising your story will take time, dedication and persistence – perhaps more than you initially expected. Continue your regular writing/revision sessions as you work through the activities in this chapter. You will find that there are many organizations and individuals willing to offer support, advice and expertise while you further develop your writing talents and the project you are focused on.

Patience pays off

You may be very excited at the prospect of finding a publisher, but you will be better served by investing more revision and research time before you take that step. Your work must be truly outstanding to catch an editor's eye. By sending it out before it is ready, you are reducing its chances of ever being published.

So how do you know whether your work is as strong as it can be – or if you are simply tired of working on it? Once again, try setting it aside for a period of time so that you gain some objectivity. Put it away for several weeks this time. If you honestly find nothing that needs improvement when you take it back out, then you may have taken the piece as far as you are capable of taking it.

But you may recognize it will be quite some time before you are ready to submit your work. The activities described in this chapter will provide you with support, inspiration, learning opportunities and connections to the bigger world of children's books, until that day arrives that you are ready to take the next step.

Find your own kind

Key idea

Other writers will understand your struggles and ambitions in a way that non-writers won't. And it can be helpful to hear feedback on your work from someone who reads with a writer's eyes and thinks like a writer thinks.

Writing partners or writing groups are a chance for you to connect and share feedback with other writers. Some groups meet in person while others connect online. Some groups are more businesslike, while others lead to lifelong friendships. Some groups focus on critiquing work (sometimes also called 'critique groups'), while others function as writing support groups. You may not yet know other writers, particularly those writing children's books, but this chapter will provide you with many different ideas for ways to meet them. As you do, keep the possibility of identifying a writing partner, joining an existing writing group, or forming your own group in mind.

Becky Levine, from *The Writing & Critique Group Survival Guide*

'I believe strongly that, if you are starting your own critique group, you should – unless you know several writers very well – start that group with one other writer. Throwing too many ingredients into the critique pot all at once, without having specific guidelines and critique patterns, is a recipe for disaster. You and one other compatible writer can work together to get the core of the group established and then gradually invite other writers to join. Two people is a group – a small one that supports healthy growth.'

The benefits of writing groups

There are several potential advantages to working with a writing group. The group can provide valuable input on your work-in-progress. When it is proving difficult for you to remain objective about your story and identify what kinds of revision it needs, your writing group can provide that objective voice. They may be in the best position to help you determine whether your work is ready to be submitted to publishers.

Other writers will likely have a strong appreciation for your writing dreams. Your family and friends may grow tired of hearing about your frustrations and struggles, but your writing group has been there themselves.

For many writers, having a deadline to meet is a great motivator – so knowing that you need to bring your next chapter to a writing group session may be the thing that gets you to the keyboard in a week when writing is tough.

How does a group share work?

If you're joining an established group, make sure to ask about their practices up front. If you are forming a new group, be open to trying different tactics until you find an effective system. As a starting point, here is some information about how I structure critique sessions for my classes. Each individual's feedback session is 30 minutes long. Writers bring copies of their work for everyone in the group. My guidelines for those selections read as follows:

- If you are writing a picture book: provide the entire manuscript, double-spaced.

- If you're writing an easy reader, chapter book or novel: You should provide material that will take approximately ten minutes to read (double-spaced). Otherwise you'll get short-changed on feedback time. If you wish, you may also provide a chapter outline or brief description of what has happened up to the point of the section you are sharing.

- Indicate at the beginning of the manuscript selection whether there are particular issues or questions you would like the group to focus on.

- When it is their turn, each writer reads their work out loud. Then we take about five minutes for the group to make written comments on the manuscript copy (to be handed back to the writer at the end). The remaining 15 minutes are devoted to oral feedback and discussion.

Establish expectations

Make it a point to regularly check in so group members can share their expectations. This can keep problems from festering. Here are some guidelines that have proven valuable in the critique group experiences I've shared:

GUIDELINES FOR GIVING FEEDBACK

- Remember you are evaluating works-in-progress, not finished pieces.
- Be thoughtful, honest and respectful.
- Always begin by pointing out strengths in the writing. Mention things that stirred a reaction in you. Where is the power in the story?
- Then point out areas that left you with questions. Where were you confused? Where were you curious to know more?
- Cite concrete examples.
- Don't try to rewrite for the author. Offer possibilities, not dictation.
- Don't fail to offer genuine feedback because you are afraid of hurting someone's feelings. However, frame things in a way that is helpful rather than hurtful. Instead of saying, 'I don't think you did a good job creating Character X,' say, 'I would love to know more about what was motivating Character X.'
- Occasionally, you will not agree with a writer's choice of material. Separate content from craft except insofar it has a direct impact on writing to fit a particular children's book category.
- Remember that you will learn a tremendous amount from analysing other writers' works-in-progress.

GUIDELINES FOR RECEIVING FEEDBACK

- Be sure to let your colleagues know what kind of feedback you're looking for. Are you at a point where you only want to know what *is* working, and not what *isn't*? Is there a specific craft element (dialogue, plot) that you want the group to focus on?
- Don't argue or try to explain your work. Ask questions if the feedback is unclear, but don't use up the critique time telling the group what you meant to say.
- Avoid becoming defensive. Make notes of all the feedback you receive. Later on, you will be able to review those notes more objectively – and you can then throw out any feedback that isn't useful.

- Look for patterns in the feedback. If several different writers voice concerns about your choice of point of view, then you will want to examine that element carefully.
- Listen for clues about where your writing is not accomplishing what you hoped. Remember that, if an adult reader is confused, then children will be, too.

WHAT TO BEWARE OF

Over the years, I have been a member of many different groups, some of which didn't work out, and others which provided the exact type of support and feedback I needed at that stage of my writing career. Just as with any other type of group experience, there can be highly effective writing groups, and those that are not a good match for you.

The most difficult dynamic I have seen is when group members' critiques take on an overly negative tone. It is best to address this in a straightforward manner as a group. Remember that it is not the job of group members to rewrite each other, but instead to point out the strengths and areas of potential growth in each work. Another thing that can happen is that a writing group can become purely social. Again, this is something for the group at large to discuss. The group may agree that they are fine with more socialization, but if some members feel it is detracting from their chance to hear feedback, then it needs to be addressed.

In the end, some writers do not find writing groups helpful. You will only know by trying for yourself. But wait to share your work at a point when you are ready for feedback. Sometimes even constructive criticism can make you lose forward momentum. And make sure you keep writing rather than just talking about your writing. Telling your group about your story ideas can be fun, but then you must carry through on getting them down on paper as well.

Structuring for success

You can structure your group to be more successful. Write up a charter defining the group's core agreements. Regularly review the document to ensure that everyone is comfortable with how things are working. Here are some of the elements to consider:

- **Time commitment:** How often will the group share work? How long will each session last? How many members' pieces will be critiqued each session?
- **Group composition:** Unless you have chosen to stick with a one-to-one partnership, you want to have enough members to account for inevitable absences, but not so many members that – based on the time commitment group members are willing to make – it takes too long to provide feedback for everyone in a reasonable timeframe (perhaps every other session?). Also, will the group be made up of writers focusing on a specific type of work only (young adult, for example), or include a mix of writers?
- **Location:** Will the group meet in person, via email, via Skype or a mix of formats? Will you meet in a public space, or at members' homes?
- **Confidentiality:** I recommend stating directly that all group members agree to keep shared work and ideas strictly confidential.
- **Sociability:** How much of the group's time will be devoted to informal conversation versus critique time versus hands-on writing time?
- **Group dynamics:** How and when should members raise concerns about the group? Who is in charge, and does leadership rotate?

Join the club

As you look to identify possible writing partners or group members, there is already a structured way for you to connect with other children's book writers around the world. The international Society of Children's Book Writers and Illustrators – commonly called SCBWI – accepts both published and unpublished writers and illustrators as members.

The organization has regional chapters and online opportunities to connect with other members, ask for advice and share news. You can visit their website at scbwi.org to find your region, inquire into the next event in your area, and learn more about the many resources SCBWI makes available.

SCBWI website

'Our mission is to support the creation and availability of quality children's books around the world. We accomplish this by fostering a vibrant community of individuals who bring books for young readers to the public including writers, illustrators, editors, publishers, agents, librarians, educators, booksellers, bloggers, enthusiasts and others. We provide education and support for these individuals through our awards, grants, programs and events. We strive to increase the quality and quantity of children's books in the marketplace, and act as a consolidated voice for professional writers and illustrators worldwide.'

Grow your writing world

Key idea

Don't despair if you live in an isolated area or if you are not an extrovert. Many writers are introverts; if this is the case for you, you will find yourself among friends. The children's book world is full of exceptionally generous and warm individuals who will go out of their way to make you feel welcome.

There are many opportunities for you to connect with the writing and book community. The Institute of Children's Literature (institutechildrenslit.com) offers writing instruction to English-language speakers around the world. Other well-known writing centres also offer online instruction. You will want to check universities and art centres for in-person classes in your area. SCBWI and other organizations periodically host children's book writing conferences, and you may find it beneficial to travel to one of these events.

Become a regular at your nearest bookstore and library. Booksellers and librarians are great sources of information about forthcoming new titles, trends and ideas about what children are asking for. Some bookshops and libraries also host public author events and readings. These are a great opportunity to ask more established writers questions about their work and to meet them in person as they autograph copies of their books for you.

You can form strong connections from the comfort of your writing desk; there is a large and extremely active children's book presence on the Internet. You can connect via chat rooms, by following and commenting on blogs, and through other forms of social media.

KidLitosphere Central (www.kidlitosphere.org), the Society of Bloggers in Children's and Young Adult Literature, provides links to numerous blogs as well as a 'sampler set' for blog beginners. The best blogs provide insightful book reviews, book industry news, interviews with editors and agents, writing tips and other kinds of invaluable information – all for free! Regularly reading your favourite blogs will serve as an ongoing form of education on the children's book world.

Online goldmine

Visit KidLitosphere Central's page that features 'A "Sampler Set" for Blog Beginners' at www.kidlitosphere.org/sampler. Scan down the list and select at least five blogs to visit today. Return as often as you can to visit the remaining blogs listed here and on the KidLitosphere members' page. And remember that bloggers will often include a list of their own favourite blogs for you to check out.

As you identify your favourite blogs, bookmark them or add them to your blog reader and then revisit them on a consistent basis. Leave comments so that the blog's author and other followers start to get to know you – this is one important way you can build your online network.

Don't forget you need to read

Of course, one of your best forms of ongoing education is to read a wide array of children's books. You will want to make sure to include many new and recent titles in the category you are targeting with your own work, as this will give you valuable insights into the kind of work that is capturing current editors' eyes.

 Reading journal

Designate a notebook or set up a computer file as a reading journal. If you are familiar with designing databases, you might find that format helpful.

Pull out the children's books you've read recently and note the key book details in your reading journal. Include title, author, illustrator, publisher, copyright year, category and anything else you can determine from the copyright page, book cover or publisher's website such as reading level and interest level. Add notes about your own opinion of the book. If you see an editor or agent's name listed (often in an author acknowledgments page), note that too. Continue to track these details in your reading journal every time you read a children's/YA book. This information will prove invaluable when you reach the stage of submitting your work to publishers.

Monitor the marketplace

 Key idea

As you move closer to submitting your work, you are shifting your perspective from the creative act of writing to the more commercial pursuit of book publishing. As you continue to read books, blogs and other information about the world of children's books, you will increase your savvy about the children's book marketplace.

The key children's book awards – the kind that are trumpeted on book covers, blogs and Facebook pages – virtually guarantee an uptick in book sales for those titles. Study award lists and read the titles to see which books are capturing this kind of attention. Ask your local librarian which review journals she relies on for children's book purchase recommendations, and seek out those journals to study the reviews for yourself. Watch bestseller lists to see which titles are garnering the most commercial attention. News stories can also affect the world of publishing: What are the educational trends that will have an impact on book purchases? How are economic factors affecting library budgets?

SCBWI publishes resources about children's publishers for their members. You can also buy guides featuring this information, or search online to find publisher lists. These are all great starting points as you set out to learn about individual publishers' personalities and tastes. Look at your reading journal – what publisher names continually pop up in connection with the books you've most enjoyed? These publishers may top your list of 'publishers to target' when you are ready to begin submitting your work.

Once you have identified individual publishers that interest you, you can visit their websites to view their new releases, catalogues and information about whether they are open to manuscript submissions. Study the publishers' online presence to gain a sense of how they fit into the bigger world of publishing. Publishers range from huge multi-conglomerates that publish a wide variety of titles to small niche presses that focus on regional, special interest markets or particular book categories. By studying the way publishers present themselves to the world, particularly by studying the books they publish, you can get a feel for where you might find the best home for your story.

See for yourself

Go to the websites for each of these three publishers. Study the way they describe themselves, the books they feature, and anything else you can find that will give you a sense of their particular publishing personalities and preferences.

- Usborne Children's Books: usborne.com
- Bloomsbury Publishing Children's Books: bloomsbury.com/uk/childrens
- Barefoot Books: barefootbooks.com

Focus point

Researching publishers, their personalities and their tastes will set you apart when you begin submitting your work. Few hopeful writers bother with this kind of careful scrutiny. But it is a key thing that will make your manuscript stand out in what is known as the 'slush pile' of manuscripts that inundate publishers' offices.

Looking ahead to submitting your work

When you are visiting publisher websites, look to see whether they post submission guidelines. They might also label these something like author guidelines or manuscript submission information. Some guidelines state that the publisher won't accept 'unsolicited manuscripts' – which means manuscripts they haven't asked to see. If this is the case, don't despair. This may make it more difficult to approach this publisher, but it isn't impossible. It is one of the areas where building your network and engaging in the children's book world can make a huge difference. For example, some editors, after speaking at a conference, will allow attendees to submit work to them even if their publishing house has a 'no unsolicited manuscripts' policy. Or perhaps you will make a connection with a more established writer who will offer to pass along a recommendation of your manuscript to his editor.

Other publishers are open to manuscript submissions. You may want to set up a notebook or database file to track them. You will also want to note what their websites say about how they want work submitted; for example, publishers may vary as to whether they are open to emailed submissions and whether they want to see your entire manuscript or just a few sample pages.

Many new writers worry over finding an illustrator before they submit their picture book. But, typically, publishers handle all the details of choosing the illustrator, often without input from the writer. Even in cases where the writer is also an illustrator, a publisher may instead choose to pair the writer with a more established illustrator for a first book. Publishers don't want copious notes illuminating your illustration ideas, either – they want to give the illustrator the freedom to have her own creative response.

Focus point

Editors are extremely interested in discovering exciting new voices. But they are inundated with thousands of manuscripts a year from hopeful writers, and have had to set up practices and systems to find the true gems. By taking the time to refine your work to the best of your ability, research appropriate publishers, and cultivate your children's book connections, you are doing the very things that will help your work stand out to these busy editors.

Think like a marketer

Getting a book published will require you to promote it to publishers and to readers. Some writers find this distasteful. Others find it intimidating. But learning how to think like a marketer is part of becoming a professional writer.

When you submit your work to a publisher, you will include a cover letter (accompanying the manuscript) or a query letter (asking an editor or agent for permission to submit your manuscript). A brief, attention-grabbing story summary is an important element of this cover letter – something that gives the recipient a tantalizing sense of your story and a hint of your voice. But you should keep this summary very succinct. It's hard to do effectively, but, with practice, you can develop this writing skill just like other writing skills!

Write a one-paragraph (no more than 150 words) promotional description of your story. Don't try to relay every plot point. Instead, key in on the core conflict and the transformation the character experiences. Focus on specific details that make your story unique and that will grab an editor's attention. Remember that editors will be looking to see if your story has appeal for a particular children's book category.

To study examples, pull some of your favourite books off of your bookshelves and review the promotional copy on the jacket flap or back cover. Reading these promotional pitches for published books can be a great way to learn how to write one for your own manuscript.

Here's the cover letter summary for my middle grade novel *Turn Left at the Cow* – it's certainly not perfect, but it gives you an idea of what to strive for with the above activity:

'Thirteen-year-old Trav knows he can never fit in with his new stepfather. So when he sees a catfish walk out of its pond on TV, he decides to follow suit and go searching for the place where he truly belongs. But his escape to the small town where his real father grew up, and his grandmother still lives, doesn't go as expected. His first day there he finds an apparent human head in Gram's freezer, and then discovers that his long-dead father was a bank robber. Soon the town deputy accuses Trav of knowing the whereabouts of the missing bank loot. With the help of the girl-next-door and her cousin, Trav sets out to find the money and clear his name – a search that escalates into a matter of life or death. The outcome requires Trav to develop a new understanding: that belonging involves both accepting and being accepted.'

Considering your work through marketing eyes can also help you with the writing and revision process. It forces you to consider whether your manuscript will have appeal for your target readers. If encapsulating your story in a tantalizing way is especially difficult to do, it can be a sign of key revision concerns. Your story may lack focus or a core conflict. You may identify holes in your plot or find that you lack a character transformation. You may recognize that your story doesn't hold any surprises.

Focus point

Part of selling your manuscript to a publisher will include promoting yourself as a children's book writer. Make sure that your current online presence – your website, blogs, Facebook page – all reflect positively on you. Editors who are seriously interested in your manuscript may Google your name to learn more about your background. You want to avoid them discovering anything that might signal that you will be a hard sell to parents looking for books for young children.

The role of agents

Literary agents pitch manuscripts to editors for the writers they represent. They also negotiate contracts on their authors' behalf and work with writers to help them shape their careers. Obviously, a good agent can be a real asset to a writer, especially in the submissions process. The problem is, it is often just as hard to find an agent as it is to find a publisher. And not all agents represent children's books – particularly books targeting the younger categories. So, depending on what category you write for, finding an agent might actually be tougher than finding a publisher.

The good news is that while an agent can be very helpful, it's not mandatory that you have one to get published. For now, you will want to track information about agents in the same way that you are tracking publishers and editors. Note agent names when you find them connected to the books you've most enjoyed. Search online for agent interviews and blogs. Look for conferences where agents are speaking or offering feedback on manuscripts. Searching for an agent is very much like searching for an editor or publisher, and you will want to take the same care with polishing your manuscript and researching agents' tastes.

Children's/YA literary agent Jennifer Laughran

'Folks often shoot themselves in the foot by not taking the time to craft an effective pitch, or to target agents specifically, or to query in small batches. They submit material that is deeply flawed, not revised, not finished, or in some cases not even started. They submit material that is totally inappropriate and not what I represent...'

Don't get taken in

There are con artists who prey on people who dream of becoming published writers. The key is to do thorough research and use good judgement before paying for anything. Reputable agents, for example, do not typically charge authors a fee – they earn their money off commissions on the sales they make of authors' work. So, if an agent wants to charge you something, make sure you understand exactly why there is a fee involved. There are also 'publishers' who will tell you that they have accepted your book for publication and then charge you for their services. Traditional publishers do not charge authors a fee. There are companies that sell self-publishing services (more on that in Chapter 10), but make sure you have a clear understanding of exactly what you are paying for any time someone wants to charge you – this is not the norm for traditional publishing and agency relationships.

Create your networking plan

You want to begin building your children's book connections now for all of the many reasons we've discussed in this chapter. But you also want to achieve a balance between the time you invest in networking and the time you devote to writing and revising.

Go back over this chapter and select at least three networking activities you are going to try. Set specific goals for these activities and write them down as a commitment to yourself. For example, you might set a goal to identify a writing partner within the next six weeks, to find and regularly read five children's book bloggers each week, and to read at least one children's book each week.

Pull out your calendar and decide how and when you will schedule these activities. If your availability is extremely limited and you can only find time to do them if you take away from your writing commitment, then decide what percentage you will spend on writing and what percentage you will spend on networking. I recommend devoting at least 75 per cent of your designated 'becoming a children's book writer' time to writing/revising.

Continue to try a variety of activities and ways to balance them with writing time over the next few weeks. Which activities are the best fit for you? Which ones do you want to try as a personal challenge even though they might be more difficult for you to pursue? As you carry through on trying the activities, what benefits are you noticing?

Workshop

1 Review

For the 'Think like a marketer' activity, you wrote a one-paragraph promotional description of your story. Considering all that you have learned so far, rate your description on the following (1 being the lowest score, 10 being the highest):

- My description is framed around the character's core conflict and transformation.
  1 2 3 4 5 6 7 8 9 10

- My story sounds fresh and original.
  1 2 3 4 5 6 7 8 9 10

- My description provides clues as to the story's appeal for a particular audience.
  1 2 3 4 5 6 7 8 9 10

- My description hints at the voice of my story.
  1 2 3 4 5 6 7 8 9 10

2 Close-up

My description is framed around the character's core conflict and transformation

- Is it apparent what my main character deeply desires?
- Do I hint at the transformation my character experiences?
- Do I avoid simply stringing together plot points in a boring fashion (such as a listing of 'and then this happens')?
- It is clear the story has a beginning, middle and end?

Bearing in mind your response to the questions above, what could you change in your description to make your story sound more complete and compelling? Modify the description accordingly.

My story sounds fresh and original

- Have I used intriguing details that are specific to my story?
- Does my description include something surprising or unexpected?

- Have I represented the unique way my manuscript brings to life a familiar storyline or a common childhood desire?
- Is my description likely to be described as attention-grabbing?

Bearing in mind your response to the questions above, what could you change in your description to make your story sound fresher and more original? Modify the description accordingly.

My description provides clues as to the story's appeal for a particular audience

- Does my description include a conflict that will resonate with children of a particular age?
- If included in the story, have I mentioned the main character's age?
- Are the chosen details appropriate to the target audience?

Bearing in mind your response to the questions above, what could you change in your description to make your story sound like a better fit for a particular audience? Modify the description accordingly.

My description hints at the voice of my story

- Does the tone of the description give a sense of the tone of the overall story?
- Does the description reveal a glimpse of my personality (quirky, edgy, humorous, lyrical)?
- Have I revealed something of my voice without it reading as over the top?

Bearing in mind your response to the questions above, what could you change in your description to better hint at the voice of the story? Modify the description accordingly.

3 Re-review

Now read your revised work and re-rate the following from 1 to 10:

- My description is framed   [1] [2] [3] [4] [5] [6] [7] [8] [9] [10]
  around the character's
  core conflict and
  transformation.

- My story sounds fresh and original. 　1 2 3 4 5 6 7 8 9 10
- My description provides clues as to the story's appeal for a particular audience. 　1 2 3 4 5 6 7 8 9 10
- My description hints at the voice of my story. 　1 2 3 4 5 6 7 8 9 10

Where to next?

You have been working diligently on completing a story for children, and have started to build connections that might someday help you launch it into the bigger world of children's books. But the world of writing for children holds many other opportunities as well! We'll explore just a few of them in our final chapter.

10

Investigate other opportunities

In this guide, you've focused primarily on writing fiction in book form for young readers. Hopefully you have made solid progress on writing your children's story and are enthusiastic about continuing to refine your skills!

But, before we wrap up our exploration of the world of writing for children, I wanted to introduce you to some other exciting alternatives. We'll touch on other approaches to storytelling, as well as non-fiction, non-book and other creative possibilities that await you if you choose to move forward in this exciting endeavour!

Focus point

Many writers enjoy trying different forms and genres and writing for different audiences; it allows them to challenge themselves and to continue to think creatively.

Thinking forward

At this point, you may or may not have finished your first children's manuscript. Either way, you have learned a tremendous amount about writing for young readers and have sharpened your writing skills.

My writing students often report to me that they lose momentum when a class ends. They no longer have class sessions as a regular reminder about their goal to write for children, and they allow themselves to become distracted. I don't want that to be the case for you as you finish this guide! I hope that you will move forward with continued enthusiasm and a new-gained sense of confidence.

One way to keep your enthusiasm high is to plant the seeds of an exciting new book project. With that kind of temptation pulling at you, it is hard to allow yourself to become too distracted. You might be at the exact point where you're ready to tackle something new. You might be still immersed in the project you've been focusing on – but, in that case, remember that there are advantages to having multiple projects in your writing pipeline. Either way, I encourage you to dream ahead with a new book concept as incentive to keep writing.

Review the ideas you generated while working through Chapter 2. Hopefully you have also continued to add to your Ideas List. I have found that once I am immersed in writing, good ideas tend to pop up at all sorts of unexpected moments. You will also want to read over your Great Bits file and the wonderful nuggets you had to delete during the revision process because they weren't a good fit for that project.

Consider all of these possibilities and any others that occur to you now, and write up a brief concept for a new story. Here are some questions to consider as you do so:

- What children's book category do you plan to target?
- What theme might this new piece explore?
- What is the core conflict?
- What do you know about the main character?
- Where is the story set?

If you're also an artist

Key idea

Illustrating a book is not just about creating enticing artwork. Illustrators must be able to tell a story through pictures: your pictures must follow characters through a narrative. All of the things that you learned about storytelling in this guide will come in handy if you pursue illustration work.

This guide has focused on writing children's books. But what if you're also an artist – should you plan to do your own illustrations? What are the best tactics? You will likely need another whole guide to answer those questions, but here are some things for you to keep in mind:

- **Publishers don't expect writers to provide illustrations:** Often, publishers prefer to match writers with illustrators of their own choosing. They do not expect writers to provide their own artwork or to acquire artwork from a friend or family member.
- **Illustrators' work must be at a professional level:** If you would like to become an illustrator as well as a writer, you will want to make sure that your artistic skills are honed to the level of professionalism that editors expect. Just as you have invested time and energy working through this guide to learn how to refine your writing skills, you should do the same with your

illustrating skills. If your art is not at a professional level, you are much better off submitting your story without artwork.

- **Publishers sometimes pair new writers with more established illustrators:** This can prove true even when a new writer is also a promising illustrator. It is primarily a sales consideration. An established illustrator brings an existing audience to the work that a new writer hasn't yet cultivated. Pairing the two makes marketing sense for the publisher.

- **You are part of the community, too:** Illustrators are an important part of the children's book community. All of the information we covered in regards to networking and tapping into the children's book community applies to illustrators as well.

- **Illustrators create a different kind of dummy:** The book dummy that we created in Chapter 8 is a tool for revising your writing. Illustrators create a much more elaborate dummy as part of their process; if you are an illustrator, you will want to research illustrators' dummies.

Graphic novels

 No Flying No Tights website

'The shortest definition of a graphic novel is this: a book-length comic.'

Graphic novels have been gaining enormously in popularity. Although they are extensively illustrated, these aren't picture books – they are typically much longer, for one thing.

Some popular books are converted into graphic novel form, but many graphic novels are original works. It is another whole arena for you to explore if you are a fan of comics, or if you are drawn to the idea of having your text illustrated but want to write for an older-than-picture-book audience. And graphic novels go far beyond the superheroes so many associate with comics; they tackle a wide range of topics, including non-fiction.

Children's magazines

Key idea

There are numerous children's magazines, and most of them publish multiple issues per year, so they need regular content from writers.

Most writers come to writing for children with the hope of seeing their name on a book cover. But magazines are another key market for children's writers.

Just as book publishers target specific audiences based on children's age ranges, so do magazines. Many of them also appeal to special interests such as science or pop culture. You can study magazines in much the way you studied book publishers to get a sense of their personalities and tastes.

Chapter 8 mentioned that sometimes writers mistake their very short pieces for picture books when they are actually short stories better suited to magazines. One way to tell is if your story has only a few illustration possibilities, and yet seems complete – short stories are not the same partnership of text and illustration that picture books are, and magazine stories will likely be accompanied by only one or two illustrations. Another clue is if the story's subject is a better match for readers older than typical picture book listeners.

Along with stories, magazines also rely on writers to provide craft ideas, puzzles, non-fiction articles and poems (more about poetry and non-fiction follow). And if you do get something published in a magazine, it serves as a great writing credit that you can claim when you pitch your book manuscripts to publishers.

 ## Minding magazines

Highlights for Children is one of the best-known US magazines for children. Visit this link to see their contributor guidelines: highlights.com/contributor-guidelines. Then Google 'children's magazines' and spend some time exploring the many other possibilities. You can add a geographic specification such as 'children's magazines UK' if you wish to narrow your search. When you find a magazine that interests you, note the target readers' age levels, the magazine's focus or special interest, and what they say about writers submitting their work.

Non-fiction

 ## Focus point

Non-fiction books make up a significant portion of the titles published for children. Perhaps your entry into writing for children is not through writing stories, but through making factual information come alive for young readers.

Some writers make a career out of writing non-fiction for children. Both children's books and magazines are outlets for non-fiction writing. And studies seem to indicate that many boys prefer non-fiction to fiction.

Broadly, non-fiction titles fall into three categories: information, inspiration or entertainment. But the categories aren't mutually exclusive; titles that fit into the information category can also be highly entertaining. They require great creativity on the part of writers and add the demand of scrupulous research (remember to review the rules for research laid out in Chapter 5). You can find non-fiction for all the same children's book categories that we covered for fiction, from picture books through young adult.

If you are interested in writing non-fiction, make sure to read a wide variety of current non-fiction titles, as contemporary titles are presented quite differently than their older counterparts. Study publishers' books and guidelines to see where there are differences from how they approach fiction – for example, non-fiction picture books can generally get away with a higher word count than fiction picture books. But, despite what differences you may identify, many of the best non-fiction titles follow the same writing rules as good fiction: they tell a compelling story. It might be a true tale about a real historical event, or a narrative about how scientists are searching for an answer to a real-life mystery, but it is still a story.

Educational publishers

Key idea

Some non-fiction books are published by the same publishers you are likely to approach with your fiction manuscripts (referred to as trade publishers), whose titles are sold through venues such as bookshops. Other non-fiction titles – published by what are called educational publishers – are created to support the school curriculum and are less likely to be found in bookshops.

The books published by educational publishers are not traditional textbooks, but titles such as biographies, explorations of scientific topics, or books that explore cultural phenomena – books that will be used by students doing research or for further reading in school. Educational publishers also publish high-interest titles with the intention of appealing to reluctant readers, young people who aren't typically engaged by books. These might include books about monsters or sports, joke books or activity books.

As we discussed in Chapter 2, schools are an important part of the children's book market for both trade and educational publishers. Savvy non-fiction writers carefully examine curriculum standards to identify possible book topics. Or, a writer who has particular expertise – for example, academic training in archaeology or hands-on experience with car racing – might decide to write a children's book about that topic.

Educational publishers also study the curriculum to identify what topics they would like to add to their offerings. They often publish books in sets – for example, a series of books where each one covers a different country of the world, or describes the characteristics of a different type of animal. Then they hire freelance writers to write one or more of the books, providing guidelines so that the various writers for that series create titles that meet the publisher's needs. If you are interested in pursuing this kind of freelance writing, SCBWI and other sources provide listings of these educational publishers. You can visit those publishers' websites to see what information they want you to provide for possible consideration as a freelance writer.

After 'the end'

Back matter, or end matter, is the material that appears after the main body of a book, and might include things such as a glossary, timeline, author's note, list of recommended books and websites, or collection of 'fun facts'. Educators and librarians value back matter, so publishers encourage writers, especially of non-fiction, to include it in their books.

Try your hand at creating a simple chart that could work as back matter for this guide: a chart listing the key steps in creating a children's book. Putting it together will serve as a useful review for you of the steps we have covered. You can go into as much detail as will be helpful for you, but, if you prefer, you can also keep it simple by including only major steps, such as:

- Step 1: Choose the children's book category you will write for.
- Step 2: Brainstorm book ideas, and so on.

Poetry

In Chapter 7, we discussed rhyming verse: how difficult it is to write well, and how effective it can be for readers when it is. But just as poetry written with adults in mind can take many forms, so can poetry for children – and there is much to be found alongside the best rhyming verse. Young people's poetry can be about a myriad of subjects and evoke a range of moods and emotions. It can avoid rhyme altogether. It can target the interests of young children or appeal to the teenage mindset.

There are picture books where the entire text is one poem, and picture books that are collections of poems. Publishers produce collections of individual authors' poems for the other children's book categories as well.

But, if you aren't yet ready for a collection, many children's magazines buy the rights to publish single poems. There are online publishing opportunities as well. And anthologies – collections of individual poems by different authors – are published around specific themes or concepts.

There are fewer poetry titles published than fiction or non-fiction, so the competition for the slots on publishers' lists is intense. But children's poets have an active online presence and work hard to cross-promote each other's work. If writing children's poetry calls to you, you will want to become a part of this dynamic online world so that you can learn about opportunities, such as anthology calls for submission, as they arise. Make sure to start following Poetry Friday, where each week a poetry blogger rounds up related posts. You can find the schedule here: www.kidlitosphere.org/poetry-friday.

Novels in verse

If you have a poetic bent, you may also want to consider writing a novel in verse. Basically, it is a story told through a series of poems, and the form has seen recent popularity growth in books for children, especially teenagers.

 ## Librarian Kelly Jensen

'Since novels written in verse are constructed with a format and style in mind, rather than a genre, they can range from contemporary stories to historical, and they can include mysteries, fantasy, science fiction, and more. Non-fiction can be written in verse, as well… [V]erse novels can be quite appealing to more reluctant readers because they're less intimidating to look at visually and because – for the most part – they read fairly quickly.'

 ## Become well-versed

Many people are unfamiliar with novels in verse. To familiarize yourself with the form, go once again to amazon.com or amazon.co.uk, and this time enter 'novels in verse' in the search bar. Scroll down the list of titles that pop up. Find at least five titles whose descriptions appeal to you – choosing those that have the 'look inside' feature available. Read the openings of those five titles to get a taste of the form and to see the way that different authors approach it.

Self-publishing

 ## Key idea

Technological advances have made it more cost-efficient to print small quantities of books, and the ebook market continues to grow. Writers have more options than ever when it comes to self-publishing.

Self-publishing is now a viable possibility for writers. And there have been a few enormously successful titles that started out as self-published books. So it seems enticing to consider this route when you are having trouble finding a publisher for your work. But you should be aware that successful self-published books are the exception rather than the rule. And, because so many self-published books are not well edited or designed, there is a stigma attached to the category overall. Many self-published writers assume that all they need to do is to create their book, and customers will appear as if by magic – which couldn't be further from the truth. So you should consider the pros and cons carefully before deciding whether this is the appropriate route for you.

If your intention is to publish a small number of books for distribution to a limited group of friends, then self-publishing offers several exciting options. Carefully research the possibilities, ask for references from the company you select, and make sure you know exactly what all the costs will be going into the process.

But, if your goal is to reach a bigger audience, then marketing and initial investment costs will be key considerations for you. Books have a relatively high production cost and consumers are not willing to pay a corresponding high price for them, so you must sell a large quantity to make any profit. Even ebooks have costs associated with them. Selling books is expensive and time-consuming. If you have a background in business management and marketing, then you may enjoy acting as a publisher – those are the kinds of tasks that make up much of a small publisher's day. But if you went into writing because you love to be creative, you might find yourself overwhelmed or bored by tasks such as managing book inventory and preparing sales materials. Make sure that you have a solid business plan and a willingness to sell and promote your work before making the investment required for any kind of self-publication where your goal is to attract an audience outside of your close connections.

Focus point

The biggest mistake most self-publishing writers make is assuming that creating the book is enough. In almost every case, to succeed as a self-published writer, you must invest a considerable amount of time, energy and money into marketing your book.

Children's book literary agent Joanna Volpe

'[T]here is a difference between "just getting your book out there" (self-pub) and having a structured business plan that includes a marketing budget, a publicity plan, and a professional editor and cover designer (indie pub).'

Keep following your dream!

If you have followed through on what this guide asks of you, you have worked hard and exerted a lot of personal energy in pursuit of the dream of becoming a writer for children. Now it's time to take all that you have learned and put it into practice on your own terms. But how will you move forward so as to keep your momentum going and your newfound writing skills sharp?

The answer is that you will want to be intentional about setting – and meeting! – writing, revising and networking goals. This guide has provided many tools and tactics you can use to continue to stretch your creative skills and learn more about the world of children's books. If you pursue the suggested networking avenues, you will continue to learn about other opportunities. The key is to find ways to motivate yourself to follow through on those opportunities.

For this activity, create a contract outlining what activities you are willing to commit to in order to continue to pursue your dream. A basic outline for a contract follows here, but feel free to adapt it to fit your own goals. Then frame it for over your desk or keep it in a place where you will regularly see it – so that your dream won't fade as so many do!

WRITING CONTRACT

Your name:

Date:

As a sign of continued dedication to my children's book writing dream, I agree to the following:

I will maintain a regular writing/revising schedule consisting of:

[If it is not yet finished,] I will complete the story I began while working on this guide.

I will continue to maintain an Ideas List where I collect intriguing possibilities for new stories, poems, or non-fiction pieces.

I will read ☐ children's/young adult books per month.

I will spend ☐ minutes per week (on average) pursuing the following activities with the goal of continuing to engage with the broader children's book community:

-
-
-
-
-

Workshop

1 Review

For the 'Thinking forward' writing activity, you wrote up a concept for a new children's writing project. Look back at what you wrote. Considering all that you have learned so far in this guide, rate your idea on the following (1 being the lowest score, 10 being the highest):

- My idea will appeal to and be relatable for children or young adults.
  [1] [2] [3] [4] [5] [6] [7] [8] [9] [10]

- My idea taps into something universal about the human experience.
  [1] [2] [3] [4] [5] [6] [7] [8] [9] [10]

- My idea has an element that is fresh or unique.
  [1] [2] [3] [4] [5] [6] [7] [8] [9] [10]

- My idea might also work in one of the alternate forms we explored in this chapter.
  [1] [2] [3] [4] [5] [6] [7] [8] [9] [10]

2 Close-up

My idea will appeal to and be relatable for children or young adults

- Is your idea something that will appeal to children or young adults?
- What would make your idea even more relatable to your target audience?
- Considering the broader context of your idea, what should you steer away from because your target audience won't be interested, or it is not age appropriate?

Bearing in mind your response to the questions above, what could you do to make your idea more appealing and relatable for children or young adults? Add your thoughts to your concept write-up.

My idea taps into something universal about the human experience

- Would children from different parts of the world be able to relate to some element of your idea?
- Would children from different socio-economic backgrounds be able to relate to some element of your idea?
- Does your idea have a 'timeless' quality – will children 30 years from now find something relatable about it?

Bearing in mind your response to the questions above, what could you do to make your idea a stronger reflection of the universal human experience? Add your thoughts to your concept write-up.

My idea has an element that is fresh or unique

- Does your idea feel generic or too broad?
- Does your idea seem too similar to other books you've read?
- Does your idea contain some attention-grabbing element?
- Is there something about your idea that might make someone say, 'I was aware that children experienced this, but I've never thought about it in quite this way (or from this point of view) before.'

Bearing in mind your response to the questions above, what could you do to make your idea feel more unique and original, or to offer a fresh take on something? Add your thoughts to your concept write-up.

My idea might also work in one of the alternate forms we explored in this chapter

(NOTE: If your idea is not a good fit for one of the alternate forms, that does not necessarily make it a bad idea. Instead, this question is included to encourage you to think outside the box about other possibilities.)

- Would your idea make an intriguing short story for a children's magazine?
- Could you imagine your story in graphic novel form?

- Is there some way to reframe your idea as a non-fiction topic?
- Could you use your idea as the basis for a poem or a novel in verse?

Bearing in mind your response to the questions above, is there an alternate form you might be interested in exploring? Add your thoughts to your concept write-up.

3 Re-review

Now read your revised work and re-rate the following from 1 to 10:

- My idea will appeal to and be relatable for children or young adults.

  [1] [2] [3] [4] [5] [6] [7] [8] [9] [10]

- My idea taps into something universal about the human experience.

  [1] [2] [3] [4] [5] [6] [7] [8] [9] [10]

- My idea has an element that is fresh or unique.

  [1] [2] [3] [4] [5] [6] [7] [8] [9] [10]

- My idea might also work in one of the alternate forms we explored in this chapter.

  [1] [2] [3] [4] [5] [6] [7] [8] [9] [10]

Where to next?

I hope this guide has given you many reasons to continue to pursue the world of writing for children. This world offers enormous creative satisfaction, and you now have the necessary tools to make many more exciting discoveries about it and your own capabilities!

It's up to you. Will your next step lead down the path of your dreams?

Celebrated children's book writer Neil Gaiman

'We have an obligation to understand and to acknowledge that as writers for children we are doing important work, because if we mess it up and write dull books that turn children away from reading and from books, we've lessened our own future and diminished theirs.'

Glossary of literary terms

ACTION

Events that take place in a story

AGENT

An individual who represents writers to publishers, submitting their work and negotiating contracts on behalf of the writers he or she represents

CHAPTER BOOKS

Fairly simple books broken into chapters for newly independent readers

CHARACTER

The person or creature featured in a story

CHARACTER ARC

The way a character transforms and grows throughout the course of a story

CLIFFHANGER

A chapter ending that concludes with a surprise or with the character in a difficult or risky position

CONFLICT

The problem or obstacles the character is confronting

COVER LETTER

A letter that accompanies a manuscript being submitted to a publisher

CRAFT

The skills that go into writing

CRITIQUE

To review and provide feedback on a writer's work, or the feedback provided

DIALOGUE

A discussion between characters

DIALOGUE TAG

An attribution indicating who has spoken (such as 'he said')

DRAFT

A not-yet-fully polished version of a written piece

DUMMY BOOK

A mock-up of a picture book used as a revision tool or to showcase an illustrator's ideas for the potential artwork

DYSTOPIA

A story that features an imagined, oppressive society

EASY READER

Short books where the language is carefully controlled for developing readers to learn reading skills

EDITOR

An individual who works with a writer to refine and polish their work

EDUCATIONAL PUBLISHER

Publishers who target the school and library market

FANTASY

A type of fiction that features magic or supernatural happenings or an imaginary or alternative world

FIRST PERSON

A point of view where a character is the narrator; it features the 'I' voice

FLASHBACK

A scene that takes place in an earlier time than the main story

GENRE

A category of writing characterized by style, form or content (e.g. science fiction)

GRAPHIC NOVELS

A novel that tells the story through illustrations as well as text and appears similar to a very long comic book

HISTORICAL FICTION
A story that features a setting of some previous time period

ILLUSTRATIONS
Artwork that accompanies a written work

MANUSCRIPT
The rough version of a written piece, before it is turned into a book

METER
The arrangement of stressed and unstressed syllables in a poem

MIDDLE GRADE
Multi-layered stories or non-fiction concepts written for readers ages 8–12

NANOWRIMO
A familiar name for National Novel Writing Month (November)

NARRATIVE
A story

NOVEL IN VERSE
A long story told through a series of poems or poetic pieces

OUTLINE
A preliminary plan for a written work

PACING
The speed at which a section of story moves

PANTSER
A writer who does not outline in advance and instead writes 'by the seat of his pants'

PARANORMAL
Books that include elements that fall outside the scope of scientific explanation

PICTURE BOOK
Short books with eye-catching illustrations that are meant to be read out loud by an adult to a young child

PLOT

The sequence of events that make up a story

PLOTTER

A writer who carefully plans out the events of her story in advance of writing it

POINT OF VIEW

The perspective from which a story is told

PROCESS

The approach by which a work is written

PUBLISHER

A company that turns a manuscript into a book and then promotes and distributes it to the marketplace

QUERY LETTER

A letter asking a publisher for permission to submit a manuscript

READING LEVEL

The complexity of a written text in regards to the skill level someone would need to be able to decode it

RESOLUTION

When the problems of the story are solved or the obstacles overcome

REVISION

Making changes to a written text to refine it and make it stronger

RHYMING VERSE

Poems or stories in poetic form where the ends of lines rhyme in a regular pattern

SCBWI

Familiar name for the Society of Children's Book Writers and Illustrators

SCENE

A sequence of continuous action

SELF-PUBLISHING

When a writer publishes or pays to have published his or her own work

SENSORY DETAILS

Details that incorporate one or more of the five senses (sight, sound, smell, taste, touch)

SETTING

The place and the time of a story

STRUCTURE

A story's foundation

SUBMISSION

The process of sending a manuscript to a publisher for consideration

THEME

The deeper meaning that unifies the story, revealing some truth or insight about human experience

THIRD PERSON

A point of view choice where there is an outside narrator who refers to the characters as 'he', 'she' or 'them'

TRADE PUBLISHER

A publisher who distributes their books through retail channels such as bookstores

UNSOLICITED MANUSCRIPTS

Submissions from writers that publishers have not requested

VIEWPOINT CHARACTER

The individual in the story through whose perspective readers view the action

VOICE

The unique way that a writer puts together words, a reflection of their personality, background, outlook on life and language use

WORD COUNT

The number of words in a manuscript

WORKSHOP

To review and critique a manuscript-in-progress with the aim of strengthening it, often done as a group process in academic settings

WORLDBUILDING

The development of the universe of a story, inventing or specifying physical details as well as the operating logic of the society and any other rules that dictate the way the action will unfold

WRITING GROUP

A collection of writers who meet to share their work, support each other, or to write together

YA

A familiar way of saying 'young adult'

YOUNG ADULT

Books that often feature intense stories about some element of the teen experience and that target a teen audience

Further reading and useful resources

Books

Bane, Rosanne. *Around the Writer's Block: Using Brain Science to Solve Writer's Resistance* (Jeremy P. Tarcher/Penguin, 2012).

Longtime creative coach and writing teacher Rosanne Bane offers helpful advice and many practical tips for establishing productive writing habits and defeating writer's block and other forms of creative resistance.

Kole, Mary. *Writing Irresistible Kidlit: The Ultimate Guide to Crafting Fiction for Young Adult and Middle Grade Readers* (Writer's Digest Books, 2012).

Former children's book agent Mary Kole offers helpful advice for writers looking to create and refine longer works for children and teens, all with an eye towards meeting publishers' expectations for saleable manuscripts.

Lamott, Anne. *Bird by Bird: Some Instructions on Writing and Life* (Pantheon Books, 1994).

Bestselling writer Anne Lamott offers honest and often humorous insights into living as a writer and managing to make forward progress despite the mental roadblocks creative people often place in their own paths.

Lerner, Betsy. *The Forest for the Trees: An Editor's Advice to Writers, Revised and Updated Edition* (Riverhead Books, 2010).

Former editor and current agent Betsy Lerner shares her insider's perspective on different writer personalities and the realities of the publishing world, and offers cogent advice to writers who want to get published.

Mogliner, Alijandra, and Tayopa Mogliner. *Children's Writer's Word Book*, 2nd edition (Writer's Digest Books, 2006).

This helpful guide is a thesaurus-like reference book where you can look up a word and see the school level at which a child typically comprehends it and then choose from alternate word choices suggested for other school levels.

Oliver, Mary. *Rules for the Dance: A Handbook for Writing and Reading Metrical Verse* (Houghton Mifflin, 1998).

Well-known poet Mary Oliver delivers key advice to writers who want to write metrical poetry, including rhyming verse.

Other resources

KidLitosphere Central: The Society of Bloggers in Children's and Young Adult Literature: www.kidlitosphere.org

This society's helpful website offers writers an easy way to identify and link to many of the key bloggers who are now so instrumental in helping to promote books and authors and in following the most recent developments in the world of children's and young adult books.

Mentors for Rent Facebook page: facebook.com/MentorsForRent

My business partner and fellow children's book writer Laura Purdie Salas and I offer regular tips about writing and publishing children's and young adult books on this Facebook page associated with our consulting/critiquing business.

Renaissance Learning:

Visit the company's ATOS Analyzer to plug in a manuscript and learn its reading level: renlearn.com/atos/analyze.aspx?type=1

Visit the company's BookFinder to look up comparison book titles and learn their reading levels and word counts: arbookfind.com / http://www.arbookfind.co.uk/

Society of Children's Book Writers and Illustrators (SCBWI): scbwi.org

A membership organization that offers many resources, events and other opportunities for individuals who write or illustrate children's and/or young adult books; open to both published and unpublished writers.

References

Introduction

White, E.B. 'E. B. White: The Art of the Essay No. 1'. Interview with George Plimpton and Frank H. Crowther. *Paris Review* (accessed 2 Jan. 2014). http://www.theparisreview.org/interviews/4155/the-art-of-the-essay-no-1-e-b-white

Chapter 1

Frederick, Heather Vogel. 'Discussing the Books We've Loved: Déjà Vu'. Interview with Vicki Palmquist. *Children's Literature Network* (17 Oct. 2013). http://www.childrensliteraturenetwork.org/blog/readingahead/2013/10/discussing-the-books-weve-loved-deja-vu/

Underdown, Harold D. *The Complete Idiot's Guide to Publishing Children's Books*, 3rd Edition (Penguin Group, 2008).

Alter, Alexandra. 'See Grown-ups Read'. *Wall Street Journal* (5 Dec. 2013). http://online.wsj.com/news/articles/SB10001424052702304854804579236102686324842

L'Engle, Madeleine. 'Madeleine L'Engle'. *Crosswicks Ltd* (accessed 2 Jan 2014). http://www.madeleinelengle.com/

Kuehn, Stephanie. 'So You Want to Read YA?' *Stacked* (17 June 2013).

Chapter 2

Hautman, Pete. 'Edginess in YA Novels'. *Adventures in YA Publishing* (14 Aug. 2013). http://www.adventuresinyapublishing.com/2013/08/edginess-in-ya-novels-by-pete-hautman.html

Notari, Debbie. 'What Is Theme in Literature? Definition, Examples & Quiz'. *Education Portal* (accessed 2 Jan. 2014). http://education-portal.com/academy/lesson/what-is-theme-in-literature-definition-examples-quiz.html#lesson

Bauer, Marion Dane. *A Writer's Story: From Life to Fiction* (Clarion Books, 1995).

Chapter 3

Feeney, Nolan. 'The 8 Habits of Highly Successful Young-Adult Fiction Authors'. *Atlantic* (22 Oct. 2013). http://www.theatlantic.com/entertainment/archive/2013/10/the-8-habits-of-highly-successful-young-adult-fiction-authors/280722/

Peck, Richard. Interview. *The ABCs of Writing for Children: 114 Children's Authors and Illustrators Talk about the Art, the Business, the Craft & the Life of Writing Children's Literature,* comp. Elizabeth Koehler-Pentacoff (Quill Driver Books/Word Dancer Press, 2003).

LaRochelle, David. *The Best Pet of All* (Dutton Children's Books, 2004).

Stiefvater, Maggie. *The Scorpio Races* (Scholastic Press, 2011).

Chapter 4

McCutcheon, Pam. 'Dialogue Tips'. *Pam McCutcheon aka Pamela Luzier*. 1996. http://home.pcisys.net/~pammc/dialogue.htm

Collins, Suzanne. *The Hunger Games* (Scholastic Press, 2008).

Rowling, J.K. *Harry Potter and the Sorcerer's Stone* (Arthur A. Levine Books, 1998).

Chapter 5

Erdrich, Louise. *The Birchbark House* (Hyperion Books for Children, 1999).

Marchetta, Melina. *Jellicoe Road* (HarperTeen, 2008).

Schumacher, Julie. *Black Box* (Delacorte Press, 2008).

Rylant, Cynthia. *The Relatives Came* (Bradbury Press, 1985).

Cashore, Kristin. *Graceling* (Harcourt, 2008).

Chapter 6

Zusak, Markus. 'Why I Write'. Interview with Sarah Kinson. *Guardian*. 28 March 2008. http://www.theguardian.com/books/2008/mar/28/whyiwrite?CMP=twt_gu

DiCamillo, Kate. 'Transcript from an Interview with Kate DiCamillo'. Interview with Reading Rockets. *WETA Public Broadcasting*. accessed 2 Jan. 2014. http://www.readingrockets.org/books/interviews/dicamillo/transcript/

Cameron, Julia. *The Right to Write: An Invitation and Initiation into the Writing Life* (Jeremy P. Tarcher/Putnam, 1998).

Bane, Rosanne. *Around the Writer's Block: Using Brain Science to Solve Writer's Resistance* (Jeremy P. Tarcher/Penguin, 2012).

'Press'. *National Novel Writing Month* (accessed 16 Mar. 2014.) http://nanowrimo.org/press

Chapter 7

Anderson, Laurie Halse. *Speak* (Farrar Straus Giroux, 1999).

MacLachlan, Patricia. *Sarah, Plain and Tall* (Harper & Row, 1985).

Block, Francesca Lia. *Weetzie Bat* (Harper & Row, 1989).

Dahl, Roald. *Matilda* (Viking, 1988).

Puckette, Madeline. '40 Wine Descriptions and What They Really Mean'. *Wine Folly* (13 Apr. 2012). http://winefolly.com/tutorial/40-wine-descriptions/

Chapter 8

Lamott, Anne. *Bird by Bird: Some Instructions on Writing and Life* (Pantheon Books, 1994).

Backes, Laura. 'Tips for Revising Your Manuscript'. *Children's Book Insider* (accessed 2 Jan. 2014). http://write4kids.com/feature4.html

Kole, Mary. 'How Much Revision Is Normal?' *Kidlit.com* (20 May 2009). http://kidlit.com/2009/05/20/how-much-revision-is-normal/

Chapter 9

Levine, Becky. *The Writing & Critique Group Survival Guide: How to Give and Receive Feedback, Self-Edit, and Make Revisions* (Writer's Digest Books, 2010).

'Mission'. *Society of Children's Book Writers and Illustrators* (accessed 2 Jan. 2014). http://www.scbwi.org/about/mission/

Laughran, Jennifer. 'How to Get Your Children's Book Published'. Interview with David Henry Sterry. *Huffington Post* (10 Jan. 2011). http://www.huffingtonpost.com/david-henry-sterry/the-inside-skinny-on-kids_b_806300.html

Chapter 10

'Definitions'. *No Flying No Tights* (accessed 2 Jan. 2014). http://noflyingnotights.com/comics-101/definitions-vocabulary/

Jensen, Kelly. 'Get Genrefied: Verse Novels'. *Stacked* (2 May 2013). http://www.stackedbooks.org/2013/05/get-genrefied-verse-novels.html

Volpe, Joanna. 'Long Term Query Do's and Don'ts Tip: Your Decisions Now DO Affect Later Relationships'. *Pub(lishing) Crawl* (10 Dec. 2013). http://www.publishingcrawl.com/2013/12/10/long-term-query-dos-and-donts-tip-your-decisions-now-do-affect-later-relationships/

Gaiman, Neil. 'Why Our Future Depends on Libraries, Reading and Daydreaming'. *Guardian* (15 Oct. 2013). http://www.theguardian.com/books/2013/oct/15/neil-gaiman-future-libraries-reading-daydreaming

Index